HATCHES & FLY PATTERNS
of the
GREAT SMOKY
MOUNTAINS

HATCHES & FLY PATTERNS
of the
GREAT SMOKY MOUNTAINS

DON KIRK

WILLIAM MCLEMORE

HEADWATER
BOOKS

STACKPOLE
BOOKS

Published by
STACKPOLE BOOKS
5067 Ritter Road
Mechanicsburg, PA 17055
www.stackpolebooks.com

Printed in the United States of America

10 9 8 7 6 5 4 3 2 1

FIRST EDITION

Cover design by Caroline Stover
Cover photo by Louis Cahill

Library of Congress Cataloging-in-Publication Data

Kirk, Don, 1952-
    Hatches & fly patterns of the Great Smoky Mountains / Don Kirk. — First edition.
        pages cm
    Includes bibliographical references and index.
    ISBN 978-0-8117-1117-3 (pbk.)
    1. Flies, Artificial—Great Smoky Mountains (N.C. and Tenn.) 2. Fly tyers—Great Smoky Mountains (N.C. and Tenn.) 3. Nymphs (Insects)—Great Smoky Mountains (N.C. and Tenn.) I. Title. II. Title: Hatches and fly patterns of the Great Smoky Mountains.
    SH451.K44 2014
    799.12'40976889—dc23
                                                                    2014009599

Contents

J DUKE

Foreword

According to Ezekiel in the Old Testament, there is nothing new under the sun. Nothing anyone can say better applies to the trout flies used by fly fishermen over the centuries. If you held out your hand, I could drop a dozen flies into your outstretched palm, each with a different name, and odds are you could not tell one from another—unless of course you tied them yourself. Differences between patterns can vary from being virtually nonexistent to being as slight as the gauge of thread or a slight difference in the shade of dubbing.

Nonetheless, the minuscule difference between one fly pattern and another is an inseparable component of fly fishing. Knowing more about flies or being able to produce works of art at a fly vise does not always translate into a more successful fly fisherman. For some, tying expands their love of the sport. For others it supersedes

Great Smoky Mountains National Park has over 600 miles of trout holding streams. WILLIAM MCLEMORE

their actual interest in fly fishing. The best anglers find a balance. If you don't have at least a curious fascination with these shrouded-hook deceivers you had better learn to catch trout well, because flies and their failure to perform are great excuses for getting out-fished.

If you are still reading this, two things are evident: you have already bought the book (or at least checked it out of the library), and you are likely a fly fisherman with an extra helping of curiosity about the whys and whens of flies and fly patterns. You've probably already purchased a fly vise and have several neatly ordered boxes containing a "zern" of feathers, fur, thread, hooks, and surgical-looking tools. No doubt your investment in fly tying is more substantial than your family can readily comprehend.

It is not uncommon for many well-meaning fly fishermen to transition into fly tiers. It happened to me in my teens, and over the years the practice was quite instrumental in helping me along during extended periods of therapy. Not so long ago, fly tying was necessary not only to save money, but also to ensure you had the correct fly for where you were fishing. In the vicinity of the Great Smoky Mountains this was especially true. Here, some seventy-five years ago, a cadre of enterprising tiers not only began creating fly patterns for profit, but also helped improve their catch rates.

The purpose for this book and for compiling the randomly scattered tidbits of fly information (sociologically speaking of course), is to once and for all settle the question of flies of the Great Smoky Mountains. Having said that, please let me add that I am currently working on a second volume on the subject. Over the years I have met lots of fly tiers, young and old, and I've been lucky enough to meet at least a few of the *real* old timers as well. To the man, they all had opinions on what fly does this or that, and where it originated. When you toss in the variations that come and go depending on the sobriety of the tier, well, you find that a lot of patterns have pretty fluid pedigrees. "Who fathered this fly or that fly?" gets mixed with "Who adopted it?" along with "Where did the rooster who provided the hackles live?"

Frankly, when it comes to some of the old fly patterns of the Great Smoky Mountains it so far has been very difficult, even close to impossible, to pinpoint the origins of many flies using anything more than enlightened conjecture. With this in mind, plus knowing that someone might disagree with my assessments of the flies of the Great Smoky Mountains, I have proceeded with due caution and diligence. Doubtless there will be disagreement about my conclusions, information, and speculation. For this reason you can visit www.southerntrout.com where you can post information, or for that matter opinions, beyond what is presented here.

Introduction

The landscape of fly fishing in the South, and especially in the Great Smoky Mountains National Park (GSMNP), has changed greatly since the 1970s. Those of us around in those days, not to mention the fellows we referred to then as the "old timers," marvel at the current level of popularity of fly fishing these mountain streams. I am not sure that there was a single fly shop to be found around the park in 1970, and there certainly was little in the way of written information on fly fishing there.

Locally tied flies were found in hardware stores in Newport, TN; Sevierville, TN; Bryson City, NC; and Cherokee, NC, as well as in a few gas stations and even in some of the souvenir-peddling tourist traps. Although better known then for selling shoul-

For many years the great fly fishing in the Smokies was largely unknown outside the South. LOUIS CAHILL

Despite being the most heavily visited national park, fishing pressure in the Smokies is remarkably light. WILLIAM MCLEMORE

der pads and baseball bats, the old Athletic House in Knoxville, TN, sold a large variety of flies, including those tied by local vise guru Eddy George. Likewise, Finkelstein's Sporting Goods and Pawn Shop was the fly-fishing tackle center of Asheville, NC.

In those days when tournament fishing for black bass was the rage in the region, we fly fishers were an insignificant subculture. You knew the other fly fishermen in your neck of the woods, but in this part of the world there was no such thing as Federation of Fly Fishers (FFF) conclaves, Troutfests, or consumer shows devoted to fly fishing. Back then there were perhaps half a dozen chapters of Trout Unlimited around the national park. The long battle with the Tennessee Valley Authority to prevent the destruction of the Little Tennessee River trout fishery had galvanized fly fishermen in the region, but the niceties of today, such as float boats, attractive fly shops, and guided fly-fishing trips, simply did not exist.

This is not to say that fly fishing in the Great Smoky Mountains was unknown to the rest of the world prior to that time. Many are surprised to learn that it has always been on the proverbial map. Writers from the late 1880s occasionally penned magazine articles about fly fishing there, and, even earlier, made casual entries on the subject in books. A couple books largely based on fishing in the Smokies appeared prior to 1950, but it was not until 1980 that the first comprehensive guide to fishing in the national park was published. In 1995, though, the floodgates opened. Everyone from true experts to carpetbaggers "not from around here" authored books and magazine articles on fly fishing for trout in the Great Smoky Mountains National Park, and Southern Appalachia in general. A few have even made instructional DVDs on fishing park waters. Websites and blogs devoted to fly fishing the park are thick as thieves on the Internet, surpassed only by the proliferation of fly-fishing guides and outfitters offering their services.

In the 1960s and even 1970s you might fish half a season in the national park without seeing another fly fisher. This certainly is no longer the case. Indeed, the landscape has changed, for the good and for the bad. It would be a lie on my part to say that I have not experienced considerable satisfaction watching this avalanche of interest and information over the years. Several of the old-time outdoor writers, such as Carson Brewer and Charley Elliot, lobbied me not to write a detailed guide to all of the streams in the Great Smoky Mountains National Park. They believed that a comprehensive guide to the streams of the national park would create too much fishing pressure. But obviously, if I hadn't, someone else surely would have. In fact, while writing my first guidebook, *Trout Fishing Guide to the Smokies* (1979), I knew of at least two other similar ongoing efforts by other anglers. My penance was decades of telephone calls at all hours of the day and night from anglers just wanting to talk about fishing in the park. At times it was punishment, but it was also often enjoyable.

The scariest thing related to all of this is that, in the early 1980s, I seriously contemplated opening a fly-fishing shop in downtown Gatlinburg, TN. For me, success

Many of the best fly patterns here are heavily dressed to make them buoyant. JAY NICHOLS

in such a venture would have been akin to receiving a prison sentence. As much as I enjoy perusing racks of rods and bins of flies, I can only imagine how much crazier I would be if I had been so caged up for long periods of time where I had to sell to make a profit. I shudder to think how I would have devolved as a thirty-year veteran shopkeeper, unless perhaps it was of a liquor store. My calling is writing, starting magazines, talking, and otherwise communicating a lifelong love for fly fishing for trout in the Great Smoky Mountains.

In the world of a wordsmith, providing directions to creeks and campsites is pretty simple stuff, as is explaining aquatic insects, fly tackle, tactics, and a few other things. Fly patterns are another matter. A pattern is never cut-and-dried, nor are final solutions often achieved. It is the court of contest where fly fishermen and we self-proclaimed experts on the subject of fly patterns square off to see who can produce the most impressive lists of fly names and pattern styles. As best as I can tell, the gauge for prowess is not too different from that of a bunch of little boys vying for the title of who can piss farther than his comrades. The entire affair is entertaining, occasionally enlightening, but just as often ludicrous to those who are well informed.

Well-read students of fly-fishing literature know that the first arguments documented in the sport involved fly patterns and their names and creators. I am not sure why it is true, but once a fly fisherman trades his soul for a fly vise, much of the driving motivation that hunkers them over a well-secured hook is the dream of creating a new fly pattern that outcatches any fly previous produced by *Homo sapiens*. While such efforts typically begin with the desire to create or improve an existing fly pattern for specific fly-fishing conditions, I'm willing to speculate that once a fly proves itself effective in confounding the pea-sized brain of a salmonid, the first thing many fly tiers do is name it, often after themselves or some stream to which they are emotionally attached. Like the need for food, shelter, and sex, christening a new fly pattern after oneself is found in the primeval behavior category. Hell, I am not sure how many there are, but I know that there is at least one fly registry where you can kinda sorta "patent" a pattern.

When you consider that 120 years ago it was widely believed that there were already more than 5,000 known fly patterns, one cannot help but shudder at the task set before the acceptance committee of an august organization charged with keeping up with such records and claims. Frankly, I am absolutely certain that, except for changes in fly-tying material and hook designs, the odds of a fly tier creating a new fly pattern that has not already been cast in the waters of the Great Smoky Mountains National Park are less than the chances of winning a megabucks lottery.

So why take the time to write this book? Beyond the obvious, which is to make money, sometimes I believe that I'm on a mission to pass along in a comprehensive manner what I think I know, or at least what I was told, by the experts and old timers about fly patterns. My firsthand knowledge goes back to the late 1960s, when I ferreted out fly tiers just for the opportunity to buy the flies that they created, to use on

Many remote headwater streams require so much legwork to get to that they are rarely fished. LOUIS CAHILL

my own fishing trips. Most of these men passed away decades ago and, in most instances, would never have been known much beyond their circles of fly-fishing friends had I not chronicled their talents and contributions. In retrospect, I am quite amazed that I had the presence of mind in those days to do that, as I know with absolute certainty that much of the information they shared with me was sought, not from any agenda to preserve knowledge, but merely out of curiosity and the desire to catch more trout.

This book is the best collection ever brought together to give accolades to the greatest Great Smoky Mountains fly tiers past and present. You may not agree with some, much, or anything said here about the flies and fly patterns. However, converting the masses to our message is hardly my mission. Rather it is to set the record straight and, if the good Lord is willing, to stoke the furnaces of controversy among the growing legion of fly fishermen who love trout fishing the waters of the Great Smoky Mountains National Park as much as I do.

The mission of this book is to provide as much information as possible on the flies and fly patterns used in the Great Smoky Mountains National Park. The oldest fly-fishing material referenced in the book dates to the 1840 and '50s. Every effort has been made to cover the subject of flies and fly patterns pertinent to this interest, yet the information should be closely scrutinized by fly fishermen in this region of the country. In general I regard my efforts as woefully incomplete, but I will say without making excuses that it is the most comprehensive work to date to tackle this sticky wicket. I am sure many who read this will believe otherwise about some fly patterns, and doubtless I will overlook and fail to make note of *the* most important patterns. This is why publishers put revision clauses in our contracts. If you direct your concerns to the publisher, rest assured that I will be promptly queried regarding what will be termed as a shortcoming on my part. That is how the world turns.

One of the toughest challenges of writing this book was researching the old stuff, things like very early patterns and the men who tied and fished these flies. Frankly, there is precious little written on the subject before the 1920s and '30s, and still not very much written on the subject until the 1980s. What little there is includes mostly snippets and secondhand recollections. There are a handful of us who talked to the old timers like Eddy George and Benny Joe Craig, but the real old timers like Ernest Peckinpaugh and Jim Gasque have been dead for so long that they are not even survived by their youngest fans.

My goal was to collect as much information by any means I could on the old timers and place it is some sort of time line. At best it is a starting point for the next researcher to use, validate, or invalidate. On more than a couple of occasions in the following chapters I share my best educated guesses on some flies and fly patterns. While I can honestly say that I did my best and tried to conjecture as well as any Scotsman, I am still human and making mistakes and ill-drawn conclusions is part of that particular terrestrial existence. Again, I mention your privilege to contact the publisher, who will be more than happy to extract an explanation from me.

Modern-era tiers are so classified because they are alive and among us today. As there are so many talented tiers today, it is virtually impossible to list them all, but I've undertaken considerable effort to make sure the list is as inclusive as possible. Among them are older fellows such as Walter Babb, Roger Lowe, and Kevin Howell—who were tutored decades ago by master tiers—as well as a few of the Young Turks. Some fall somewhere in between for no particular reason. My goal was completeness of material, and where possible I wanted to tell a bit about each tier, his patterns, and provide credit as best as I could where it's due in regards to fly patterns. Time and readers such as yourself will be judges of how I did.

CHAPTER ONE

The Mission: Snippets about Tippets

When it comes to some of the old fly patterns of the Great Smoky Mountains so far it has been very difficult to pinpoint the origins of many flies. LOUIS CAHILL

L ost forever is the story of the angler who first cast a fly to a trout in the waters of the Great Smoky Mountains. Doubtless the Almighty knows when and who this person was, and with scriptural evidence of the Lord's friendliness to fishermen, I freely express an opinion that it did not go unnoticed by the Creator. However, no one chronicled the event, and so the details of this occurrence are left open to wild conjecture. Unknown though this person shall remain, they must be saluted as the first to dabble a fly in these streams.

Although I am quite unconvinced that it is true, a good many people knowledgeable in such things are strongly of the opinion that the Cherokee Indians were the first fly fishermen in the Great Smoky Mountains. The subject of Cherokee fishing, and particularly with flies, has become interesting and actively discussed a good bit in recent years, with much of the credit for what has found its way into print coming from enterprising pseudoscholars on the Qualla. From my perspective, it appears that a lot more has been made of Cherokee angling for trout in mountain streams than is historically provable or logical to conclude based on the available evidence.

That catching and eating fish was important to the Cherokee of the Southern Appalachian is uncontested. What is contested is whether or not they fished with flies. It is well documented that the Cherokee used spears, seines, and weirs with deadly effectiveness. Many of the weirs they constructed centuries before in rivers such as the Nolichucky were used by white settlers well into the 1940s. Poisons extracted from pokeweed berries and the bark and roots of black walnut trees were also used often and with great effectiveness by the Cherokee. I have tried both, and they do work quite well, but not as well as hand cranking a telephone or duct taping a cherry bomb to a brick-sized rock to toss into the water. The latter is consistently effective and will bring snakes to the surface as well as any fish in the pool.

Much has been made of the local Cherokee using flies to catch trout long before the arrival of white settlers. I do not know for sure that this never happened, but I am quite skeptical of such claims for a variety of reasons. Most prominently among the reasons would have been the absence of steel/iron or bronze fishhooks to which feathers or fur could be attached. Granted, the locals had crude hooks made out of many things including the talons from hawks and owls, carved deer knuckle bones, and mussel shells. The "finest" known examples of such fishhooks that I have examined are crude and bulky, thicker than a wooden kitchen match and larger than a quarter.

Much is also made of the use of slivers of turkey wing bone that were made into nifty gadgets that opened inside the mouth of a fish when ingested. However, the ones I have examined, though delicate and impressive in terms of workmanship, could never have been made to look like a fly. Turkey bone was also used to create a tube-lure, which some sources claim was occasionally adorned with hackle. However, even if this has some validity, it would have been used after the arrival of metal fishhooks into the Cherokee communities.

Nearly all experts believe these handmade bone hooks were effective—when ingested, they securely hooked the internals of a fish. This would mean that they were shrouded in some sort of bait such as juicy nightcrawler for the fish to bite. The quarries where the Cherokee lived would not likely have harbored brook trout but bigger fish such as redhorse, drum, and other fish found in the larger, low-elevation rivers. Heidi M. Altman, in her recent book *Eastern Cherokee Fishing* noted that curiously, the Cherokee refused the catfish that are abundant in these waters. Additionally, Altman says that there is no record of flies or fly fishing at all by the Eastern Cherokee. Even if a particularly brilliant bone carver made, say, a dainty size 12 hook suitable for a fly, what would have motivated him to wrap it in hair or feathers to catch brook trout when he had methods that already worked? I think the event is quite unlikely.

The British were the first to produce modern steel fishhooks in quantities. By the mid-1500s, England was the largest producer of fishhooks in the world. Those in England who planned to go to Virginia were always advised to provide themselves with nets, fishhooks, and lines. Most hookmakers in the early years came to America from Redditch, England, and the surrounding area. That was really the center of the hookmaking world for a good many years. By the early 1600s the British, Dutch, and Swedes had well-established colonies along the Atlantic. The Eastern tribes benefitted from trade for knives, axes, weapons, cooking utensils, fishhooks, and a host of other goods. Trade between coastal and Appalachian tribes had been well established for thousands of years.

It is reasonable to suppose that iron and bronze fishhooks found their way into the possession of some Cherokee as early as the mid-1600s. This would also have been when the first horse-tail fibers could have been made available to the natives, as horses had only just begun showing up where the Cherokee lived. While I seriously doubt that the availability of these two items resulted in the immediate inception of fly fishing for trout in the Great Smoky Mountains by the Cherokee, we could argue that it occurred sometime shortly thereafter.

Fishing line is another issue. Once contact with Europeans was made, fibers from horses' tails would have been available. Prior to that, considerable evidence exists that Cherokee hemp fibers were used. John Adair mentioned the use of hemp by the Cherokee and other tribes in his *History of the American Indians* (1775). Before you get all excited about hemp, most authorities have identified "wild hemp" as wood nettle (*Laportea canadensis*) or Indian hemp (*Apocynum cannabinum*). True hemp (*Cannabis sativa*) did not become a formally recognized member of North American flora until 1606. It was first imported from Europe and introduced at Port Royal, Nova Scotia, by Louis Hebert, who was Samuel de Champlain's apothecary and botanist.

The Cherokee were quite advanced in their uses of native flora and fiber. Cattail and bulrush reeds, dogbane and wormseed plant inner fibers, the inner bark of basswood and cedar, and roots of evergreen trees were bundled or twisted into cords for weaving mats, bags, baskets, belts, or other items. The Cherokee made cord several yards long by first shredding or pounding fibrous plant material, soaking it in water, and then twisting two-plies on the thigh with the palm of the hand. Preparation of inner barks is more complicated and includes boiling the material in wood ashes to soften and separate the fibers. While these natural fishing lines probably worked well for catching bigger fish in waters such as the Tuskegee River, the leader-shy trout I have encountered would not have been so impressed.

Dried and sometimes braided animal gut might have been used as fishing line by the Cherokee, although to my knowledge there is no historical evidence of this occurring. For centuries, people from different cultures dried and twisted gut into a type of cord used for a variety of applications including fishing line. People everywhere have used the natural fiber in the walls of animal intestines, usually sheep or goat, but occasionally from the intestines of a hog, horse, mule, or donkey. It is not a great stretch to presume the pre-Columbian Cherokee had knowledge of the use of intestinal fibers of whitetail, bear, and other wildlife they relied on for protein. But to suggest that this fiber, or any other sort, was used in Stone Age fly fishing is at best enlightened conjecture.

Brook trout are the only salmonid that is native to the waters of the Great Smoky Mountains. WILLIAM MCLEMORE

It is worth noting that pre-Columbian Cherokee men defined much of their social status through hunting and warrior skills. Emptying out fish weirs might have been regarded as manly enough, but even minding gardens and cornfields was beneath the dignity of most Cherokee men. These chores were delegated to women and children. Near the Little Tennessee River is a graveyard full of my pioneer ancestors who were killed in the 1700s. It attests strongly to the fact that raising hell and making war seems to have been a passionate pastime, indeed one more so than developing fly-fishing techniques in the streams of the Great Smoky Mountains.

The use of so-called deer hair/hide flies actually has considerable historical evidence in Native American culture in the Southeast. Writing in 1741, colonial-era scribe William Bartram penned of how the Seminoles in Florida caught trout (although he was actually referring to largemouth bass). Bartram recounts that the Seminoles employed a method whereby they used a line and "bob" hook, which was a technique in practice long before the arrival of white men. Bartram was an avid sport fisherman. He is probably the first European American to catch a fish in the Southeast on an artificial bait. The Seminoles taught him how to make flies with a hook and some feathers for dangling on a pole by a stump. He called it fishing with a bob—not a bobber, but a bob. The following is what he experienced fishing with the Seminoles; it is taken from *William Bartram, 1739–1823, Travels through North and South Carolina, Georgia, East and West Florida*:

> When I returned I found my companions fishing for trout [largemouth bass] around edge of floating nymphaea [lily pads], and not unsuccessfully, having then caught what was more than sufficient for us all.
>
> Two people are in a little canoe. One sitting in the stern to steer, and the other near the bow, having a rod ten or twelve feet in length, to one end of which is tied a string line, about twenty inches in length, to which is fastened three large hooks, back to back. These are fixed very securely, and tied with the white hair of a deer's tail, shreds of a red garter, and some parti-colored feathers, all which form a tuft or tassel nearly as large as one's fist, and entirely cover and conceal the hooks; that are called a "bob." The steersman paddles softly, and proceeds slowly along shore; he now ingeniously swings the bob backwards and forwards, just above the surface and sometimes tips the water with it, when the unfortunate cheated trout instantly springs from under the reeds and seizes the exposed prey.

Once close contact had been made with the ever-encroaching, westward-bound white settlers, the Cherokee around the Great Smoky Mountains demonstrated a remarkable enthusiasm for adopting many aspects of European culture. Doubtless they were aware of recreational angling, which along with many other vices peddled by the newcomers, they partook thereof. In her 1892 book, *Favorite Flies and the Histories*, author Mary Orvis Marbury noted the following from correspondence with J. H. Stewart, dated 1887:

The streams of the Great Smoky Mountains are generally high-gradient, clear waters.
WILLIAM MCLEMORE

The two specimens of flies which I inclose you will see are reversed hackles, made by cutting narrow strips of deerskin with the hair left on, wrapped around the hook several times and well tied at each end. The North Carolina Indians tie them to perfection, using some sort of cement or waterproof varnish over the thread, and for the bodies the various colors and length of hair from different skins, bur usually rather stiff hair, preferring it from the deer's legs. They often cut the hair off and use it without the skins, but made in this way the flies are not as durable. They use feathers occasionally in the same way.

The effect of this reserve method, i.e. tying the hair to point from instead of towards the bend of the hook, is very perceptible in the swift water. Every little move in the drawing back, as the flies float down, gives the appearance of a live worm trying to get out of the water. It does not amount to much with feathers, as they have no worm or caterpillar appearance.

In addition to the forms I have send to you, they sometimes use three or more stiff hairs, running down over the curve of the hook half an inch or more, to represent the feelers on the caterpillar's head. The advantage of twisting the skin around the hook is to give a sort of twirling motion in the water as the current strikes it.

I send you specimens of hair on the skin. Trim the skin down thin, soak well in warm water, and then stretch it thoroughly, and cut into stripes to suite.

Note—The flies sent were tied in exactly the method of the recently patented "fluttering Fly," and it is claimed that these have been used by the North Carolina Indians for generations.

Interestingly, such a fly called the Fluttering Fly was patented by Abbey & Imbrie in mid-1886. In his 1889 book, *More About the Black Bass*, Dr. James A. Henshall praises the Fluttering Fly, noting that "when the fly is drawn through the water, the wings and hackle rather than closing as does an ordinary fly, expand—as is claimed, gives it a fluttering, lifelike motion similar to that of a half drowned insect." Unlike the case of the Fluttering Fly, there is little historical evidence that the Cherokee independently developed the Yallarhammar pattern, or for that matter any fly that can be rightly classified as a true fly even in terms of the most expansive definition of what we would acknowledge as a fly today, despite claims by a few writers who have wildly speculated on the subject.

When President Andrew Jackson forced the Cherokee to relocate in Oklahoma in the 1830s, a portion of the tribe fled into hiding in the remoteness that is now the Qualla Reservation. There is little doubt that much of the fishing from that point on was for brook trout and members of the sunfish family (bass and bream). War parties no longer prowled the mountain valleys, so taking a recreational fishing trip was a logical pastime. Insofar as these particular Cherokee were refugees with little legal protection, it is safe to assume that remote mountain streams became important sources of food in the form of brook trout and crayfish.

Metal hooks were more easily available then, so the tying and fishing of flies probably did occur. Doubtless with time more historical evidence will emerge on the subject of the Cherokee and fly fishing the Great Smoky Mountains. It is difficult to determine now if the influence of the native people on the subject has been over- or understated. The question of whether the first fly cast to a trout in the Smokies was by a Native American or someone of European descent probably will never be answered with certainty.

CHAPTER TWO

What Is Known about the Real Old Timers

You may feel like you are the first person to discover an inviting pool in the mountains, but the fly fishing tradition here is quite old. LOUIS CAHILL

J ust like we will likely never know the name of the first fly fisherman to sample the waters of the Great Smoky Mountains, the same can obviously be said about the first fly patterns used here, and which among them were of local origins. It seems logical to presume that the earliest flies used in the Great Smoky Mountains were wet or streamer patterns. However, there is a growing preponderance of evidence that dry-fly fishing in the streams of the Great Smoky Mountains was not far behind the development of the sport in the Catskill Mountains of New York.

Writing about angling on Raven Fork in the 1916 issue of *Forest and Field*, Donald Gillis said in an article titled "The Uncaught Trout":

> Having arrived where the water [Raven Fork] comes down crashing and flashing, slipping darkly by undermined ledges, sparkling in swift runways and lying brown in deep pools, it is to be expected that one will stop talking and go to fishing. Among my flies is one with a gold banded body and smoke colored wings. Wickhams Fancy meets the tastes of trout hereabouts. I am talking now of dry fly Wickhams; I never used the wet fly variety of this gilded deceiver. I have used the wet fly Professor and it was good; of the dry fly Professor I can cheerfully say that I never knew of anyone who ever took a trout with it. Now I am even with this flaring winged imposter for the false expectations it has often raised in me.

Better known in its wet-fly version, Wickham's Fancy is believed to have been designed by Dr. T. C. Wickham of Winchester, southern England, in the 1880s. (There is some dispute, as other Wickhams have claimed the design as theirs.) Dr. Wickham designed the fly to suggest a red spinner with wings of medium slate-gray starling feather and a body of gold tinsel over brown hackle, tied in a palmer style. The more things change, the more they remain the same, eh?

Doubtless with time more historical evidence will emerge on the subject of the Cherokee and fly fishing. Right now much of what we know is found in the form of tantalizing snippets. In William Charles Harris's much-respected *Angler's Guide Book* (written under his middle name, Charles), he notes, "The artificial fly is the universal lure favored by the native fishermen" in the Southern Appalachians. Actually, there was a lot of attention on recreational fishing in and around the Great Smoky Mountains in the 1800s.

In his 1883 book *The Heart of the Alleghanies*, Wilbur Gleason Zeigler devotes a lot of copy to trout fishing in and around the Great Smoky Mountains. However, this thorough scribe's single reference to the use of a particular fly pattern follows, although on several other occasions he alludes to the use of "flies":

> The best fishing I ever saw done was by a mountaineer, one day in early June, who used a green-winged, yellow-bodied, artificial fly with a stick-bait worm strung on the hook. As we followed down the current, at every cast of his line

he pulled a speckled trout from the water. The stick-bait is a small, white worm found in tiny bundles of water-soaked twigs along the edges of the stream. The twigs seem glued together, and when opened, reveal an occupant. In early spring, with a light sinker on your line, the common, red angle-worm on a featherless hook can be used with advantage.

Charles Lanman, a much-touted fly fisherman and travel writer, wrote in his book *Adventures in the Wilds of North America, Volume 2* of encountering "gentleman anglers" in the 1840s during a trip through the Southern Appalachians along the West Prong of the Little Pigeon and the Oconaluftee Rivers. Obviously native anglers fished these exact locations at the time Lanman made his observation, so there is some solid evidence that fly fishing by Native Americans and European arrivals was pretty well established at this time in history.

Robert L. Mason, author of *The Lure of the Great Smokies* (1927), was one of the earliest scribes to give considerable details on fishing in the Great Smoky Mountains. His well-known book provides a lengthy list of local residents who could be enlisted as guides to streams. Below is a composite of the flies and fishing advice he garnered prior to writing his book.

Most of the desirable pools for rainbow, bass, and the largest speckled trout are in sequestered locations which require much hiking or horseback riding. A night or two in the woods is the most desirable method of reaching the biggest fellows with rod and line. In the springtime it is not unusual to see mountaineers actually loaded down with strings of speckled trout. Meeting such a caravan near Reagan's store, the author, in response to a query as to fishing luck, was informed by three mountaineers in blue overalls that they had ketched about a thousand in the three days they had been on Alum Cave Prong. Big Cataloochee Creek in North Carolina, twelve miles from Mount Sterling, possibly offers the best chance for rainbow varying from one foot in length to as much as thirty inches The three branches or Prongs of Little Pigeon River also offer splendid sport for the wielder of rod and fly. These are the Right Prong, Left Prong, and West Prong, Right Prong heading toward Guyot; Left Prong toward Bull Head, and the West Prong toward Indian Gap. The fish here perhaps are not so large and plentiful as in Big Cataloochee, or even in Deep Creek, NC, and Raven Fork, and they are mostly black and striped, or "rock" bass, as termed by mountain fishermen. Speckled trout, however, are generally plentiful everywhere, and the connoisseur, who knows, likes to have a plate.

As to flies, the consensus of opinion seems in favor of the brown hackle, though with many adepts in the art it is still a moot question. Professor Karl Steinmetz (of Knoxville) has made a study of flies and he recommends, the following schedule from April to September: First preference:

Brown Hackle
Royal Coachman, or Coachman, and the Royal
Coachman Jungle-Cock, a "hybrid" fly made only by Beatty, of Butte, Montana
Cahiel [*sic*]
Cowdung
Black Gnat
Queen of the Waters
Then, in the order named:
March Brown
Montreal
Grizzly King

For all-round fishing he recommends the Brown Hackle. The Greenbrier Section of the Smokies on the West Prong of the East Fork of Little Pigeon, east of Le Conte, is also highly praised by Professor Steinmetz.

The fly (choice) varies according to the light says Charlie Gill, who has angled in practically every stream in the Smokies. A light one in the early morning; a slightly darker for noon; and a gray or black for evening. But I could always do best with a minnow tail hooked screw fashion to produce the effect of movement.

Makes no difference about the kind of fly, states Matt Whittle, an Izaak Walton of Smoky Mountain fishermen. "I've seen these mountain boys catch big ones with a bare hook practically, with every vestige of the fly gone apparently: the more ragged the better. An appearance of age always helps a fly. The manipulation has much to do with success. However, when a fellow is hungry and wants real fish with the science left out, point your flyhook with a stick-bait or wasp-nest grub and watch 'em bite."

J. F. Long, who has won many flycasting contests and is considered an expert, says: "I like a White Miller. Sometimes I use a Professor to wake 'em up when they're dead. After that, if they show interest, I run the gamut until I find one they're real hungry after. Pork rind is good for bass, especially if it has a red string in it. One must make a study of their feeding. Some scientist up here said fish were colorblind. My eye! They're artists when it comes to color!"

Billy McIntyre declares: "Brown Hackle is very good, or bucktail. The Royal Coachman is excellent, too, and the Queen of the Waters. When they are hungry you don't have to go far from these. I like a black gnat, too. Ed Akers and Henry Brandau vote for Brown Hackle, Royal Coachman, and Queen of the Waters. Don't care for a Professor especially. Too gaudy. A White Miller works very well."

A. S. Birdsong, a well-known sportsman who introduced the first game-warden law in Tennessee, says: "I have fished every nook of the Smokies, I suppose. When I want fish I use stick-bait or waspnest grubs. However, when they are hungry they will rise to chips you throw in the water. Then most any fly is good, even artificial grasshoppers. After all, a fellow must study the locality he is in. Trout are protected in spawning season. I like a fiery whipstitch of a black bass. He's interesting and sometimes will jump clear of the water after your fly."

Reuben Stinnett, mountaineer, likes a White Miller, while Reuben's father, Uncle Tip, prefers black snake-feeder (dragon-fly also known as grampus). He says, "They'll git 'em nearly every time. This is a common fly seen about mountain streams. I don't like these si-godlin things they call artificial minners. They plum scare the fish."

C. W. Standing Deer, of the Cherokee Reservation, says, "I like horsehair lines better than the commercial kinds. They don't get wet and sink. I can make a fifty-foot line in twenty minutes. It's all in knowing how to knot them so they will reel. I always bait with wasp-nest grubs I find in the bushes [in] the woods or stick-bait along the edges of streams." Standing Deer pronounces the name Smoky Mountains with something which is spelled phonetically like Guke-Tsun'ts Ga-Too'chee, the Cherokee dialect differing from ethnological bureau records of Atali'gwa Gisku Yu'sti. He claims also to be a grandson of the great Cherokee story-teller, Suye'-ta, the Chosen One, and is a great champion with the bow.

The unanimous preference for the Brown Hackle, expressed by all of the fishermen, and the statement of one of them that the line should float and not sink, suggests that the so-called bi-visible dry fly will bring the expert dry-fly fisherman a rich reward. This fly, which is now supplied in most of the best tackle shops in the North, is in essence nothing but a Brown Hackle dressed to float, with plenty of hackle and with a bit of white feather added to aid the eye of the fisherman.

Hereto overlooked in the annals of fly fishing in the Great Smoky Mountains is the influence of Ernest H. Peckinpaugh of Chattanooga, TN, prior to World War I. Many fly-fishing historians credit him with the invention of the popping bug, but seem to overlook his interest in flies for catching trout. The legend of Peckinpaugh's invention of the cork-bodied flies was recounted by Robert Page Lincoln in his 1952 book *Black Bass Fishing: Theory and Practice*:

> To E. H. Peckinpaugh, of Chattanooga, Tennessee, belongs the honor of having invented the cork-bodied bass bug. . . . According to Peckinpaugh he had accidentally dropped a cork bottle stopper on the stream which he was fishing and as it floated away with the current he was suddenly struck with the idea of making a floating bass bug out of cork. As a result he ran the stem of a hook through a cork. . . . Instead of feathers he used a pinch or two of bucktail hair, tying in the thatch at the head of the fly as it were. While this initial lure was quite crude, Peckinpaugh was amazed at the fish that it took. . . . All this took place in the year 1907.

Quite the marketer, Peckinpaugh entered into agreements with well-known anglers of the 1900s to have their names associated with special bugs and flies in his diverse line. Along with Ozark Ripley, the list includes Zane Grey and Dr. Henshall. Here's where the story gets interesting, though. Long before migrating to Chattanooga or meeting Ernest Peckinpaugh, Ripley had been in contact with none other than Theodore Gordon, the Fly Father. According to Ozark's published remarks, a letter Gordon wrote to him in 1903 indicated that the Wizard of the Neversink was dressing popping bugs prior to this time. I remain in search of the still-missing parts to this mystery of who first conceived the popping bug, but Matt Whittle's association with the country's first fly-fishing icons raises many questions that are still unanswered for those who seek a truly accurate account of the history of fly-fishing in the Smoky Mountains. It is too bad that so little was recorded or published at the time.

Peckinpaugh is best remembered for his gaudy, innovative bass bugs, but the Scenic City entrepreneur also sold loads of trout flies and was the first to commercially offer the famous Tellico Nymph. Here is a list of the flies offered in the 1920s and '30s by Peckinpaugh's line known as Floating Trout Midgets:

March Brown	Black Prince
Brown Hackle	Ginger Quill
Gray Hackle	Wickham's Fancy
Rube Wood	Cowdung
Yellow Jacket	Coachman
Stone Midget	Silver Doctor
Montreal	Yellow Sally
Paramacheene	Red Ibis
Royal Coachman	Seth Green
Black Midget	Queen of Waters
Professor	Lady Bug
Peck's Favorite	Western Bee

At the danger of approaching redundancy, but in my opinion necessary to make an important point, in Joe Manley's 1938 book, *Fishing in the Great Smoky Mountains National Park and Adjacent Waters*, the author lists the following recommended wet-fly patterns:

Plain Coachman
Gray Hackle (yellow body)
Forked Tail
Stone Fly
Hare's Ear
Dusty Miller
Cowdung
Professor
March Brown
Beaverkill

Peckinpaugh was producing and marketing trout flies almost a hundred years ago.
DON KIRK

Joe Manley also references fly rod baits, as well as other well-known fly patterns that include the Royal Coachman, Red Hackle, Parmachene Belle, Queen of Waters, Ibis, Yellow May, and "large salmon flies . . . and . . . bucktails tied with jungle cock eyes."

The point of this is to demonstrate that the flies we now refer to as traditional flies of local origins such as the Yallarhammar, Tellico Nymph, or Thunderhead are not mentioned. The only logical conclusions are that many of them had not yet come into widespread use, assuming they existed then, or that Manley and the guides quoted by Mason spoke of flies they knew would be recognized by a national readership. Personally, I think it is pretty much the flip of a coin, and that to some extent, both theories could be correct.

I am of the opinion that Joe Manley's footprints in fly-fishing lore in the Great Smoky Mountains are not only largely unknown, but by some presumably scholarly sources, virtually ignored because his books are difficult to find and he was not a self-promoter, at least by modern standards. Manley and I met and chatted on numerous occasions in the 1990s. In the 1940s and 1950s he was perhaps the best-known angler in the state, knowing outdoor writers and editors of sporting journals from many locales. Along with taking Ben East of *Outdoor Life* fly fishing on several occasions, he also accompanied Charles N. Elliott, a Georgia native and editor at the same magazine. Manley recounted frequently going fly fishing with Whittle, who he credited with showing him where and how to fish the streams of the national park. Manley says that Whittle introduced him to such famous anglers as East and Joe Brooks, also of *Outdoor Life*, as well as Ozark Ripley. Manley described Matt Whittle as the most knowledgeable angler and expert of local flora of the Great Smoky Mountains.

Whittle understood the habits of his quarry as few have on either side of the Great Smoky Mountains. Going against the common belief of his day that one had to match the hatch when fishing with flies, Whittle felt it was of no real importance what kind of fly you used, but how you fished with what you were using, and how the fish were feeding. Whittle often left his orchard-and-shrubbery business to guide "Yankee" fishermen up the streams of the Smokies. Well-known angler George La Branche is said to have been among those who accompanied Whittle into the streams of the national park.

According to Manley, one of Whittle's favorite stories involved fishing with La Branche, the noted Yankee fly-fishing expert of his era. La Branche, along with Theodore Gordon, had property (it is now inundated) along the Neversink River in New York. La Branche pioneered fishing dry flies on fast water, something new to the sport in the early 1900s. Manley mentioned that Whittle had a acquired a copy of La Branche's book, *The Dry Fly and Fast Water Fishing with The Floating Fly on American Trout Streams*. Whittle initiated correspondence with La Branche, which resulted in visits to the Great Smoky Mountains by the two most famous fly fishermen in the country.

Manley also told me that Matt Whittle also fished with Ozark Ripley, one of the best-known outdoor writers of the early 1900s, and who had moved from Missouri to Chattanooga in the 1930s. "Ozark Ripley" was actually the colorful pen name used by John Baptiste de Macklot Thompson (generally referred to as John B. Thompson), who was educated in France prior to World War I. An avid fly fisherman, Ripley lived in eastern Tennessee where he continued his passion of float fishing for smallmouth bass, a practice in which he had engaged while operating out of the Ozarks. Perhaps some very interesting Great Smoky Mountains fly-fishing lore would have come from this man's relationship with Ernest Peckinpaugh. Unfortunately, to the best of my knowledge on the subject, Ripley wrote little for publication about his stint in eastern Tennessee. As with so much of the story about southern trout fishing in those days, little was recorded to tell us what we would like to know.

A number of elements factor in to accurately establishing the origins of the earliest fly patterns of the Great Smoky Mountains. One that hinders it is the scarcity of written historical information that dates earlier than the 1920s. Clearly flies tied by local anglers around the Smokies were in widespread use prior to this time. However, recorded references of even the most vague nature are almost nonexistent. In the 1970s, when I began interviewing now-deceased fishermen like Eddy George and Walter Cole, they referenced flies shown to them by the old timers of their youth. In our conversations about fly fishing in eastern Tennessee, Eddy George often referenced a mentor named Dutch who was a fishing partner of Lou Williams, the outdoors writer for the *Chattanooga Free Press* and a well-known fly tier and maker of high-quality, split-cane bamboo fly rods. Dutch (whose last name I don't know) was a particularly salty fly fishermen in his late seventies who took George fishing with him on the Bald River in the 1930s. According to George, Dutch had the most thoroughly stocked fly boxes he had ever seen, and that most were tied by their owner. As a fifty-year veteran fly fisherman at the time, Dutch would have begun fishing these waters no later than the late 1880s.

While a little out of context with the stories of flies and fly patterns of the Great Smoky Mountains, I feel inclined to include a historical note on Lou Williams. A noted writer who covered the outdoor beat for newspapers in Chattanooga and a talented fly tier and builder of bamboo fly rods, Williams was also an ardent, politically active conservationist. A founding member of the old Tennessee Conservation League in the 1930s, he is given much credit and many accolades for his efforts to see through the passage of Tennessee's model game and fish law. He was also instrumental in the creation of the state trout hatchery along the Tellico River. A large bronze plaque commemorating him used to stand along the edge of the North River at Tellico; unfortunately, it was stolen in the late 1990s and has not been replaced, nor is it likely to be.

Walter Cole and Joe Manley both knew and fished with Matt Whittle. Whittle's time on the water dates back at least to the 1890s. Unfortunately, Cole and Manley have been dead a long time, and with them went their recollections of fly fishing in the Great Smoky Mountains and their experiences with Whittle. That recorded secondhand information from these old timers even exists about the old days and Whittle (and others) is in itself a fortunate occurrence.

Such word-of-mouth information has been instrumental in our efforts to pinpoint the genius of patterns such as the Tellico Nymph, Forky Tail, and Yallarhammar. Anything that has been or will be gleaned from such narratives, no matter how faithfully told or recorded, is still merely secondhand. Compounding this with the probable inaccuracy on the part of the original tellers renders the authenticity of entire stories tenuous at best. It is worth noting that Texas recently made it a felony for fishermen to lie about their catches, which speaks volumes about the "fish stories" for which fishermen have long been well known.

For what it's worth, my personal theory is that the old-time guides and ardent fly fishermen of the Great Smoky Mountains were initially strongly influenced by visiting Yankee anglers. Furthermore, some of them were readers of the sporting journals of the day, which promptly published the latest news in fishing techniques and flies. Interest among sportsmen with above average financial means (i.e., doctors, lawyers, professors) in the larger urban areas of the region such as Asheville, Chattanooga, and Knoxville ran concurrent with the acceptance of fly fishing by some residents of the Smokies. This group of fly fishermen exploring the streams of the Smokies was not a large group, but it appears to have been fairly close knit, at least on their respective Tennessee and North Carolina sides of what is now the national park.

I am unconvinced that what we now call traditional flies such as the Sheep Fly and Jim Charley predate the 1930s. I am of the opinion that the early tiers who preceded men like Fred Hall and Benny Joe Craig began with a tradition of copying existing fly patterns such as the Professor and the Queen of Waters, eventually morphing them into locally named patterns with their own twists in terms of dressing, design, and materials used in construction. My search continues for older evidence to the contrary, but for now this is my best guess as to where and how Great Smoky Mountain traditional fly patterns came to be.

CHAPTER THREE

How It Seems
to Have Happened

Unlike many eastern trout fisheries, the streams of the Great Smoky Mountains offer great year-round fishing. LOUIS CAHILL

Many anglers in and around the Great Smoky Mountains were not only relatively well-versed fly fishermen as much as 130 years ago, but they also tied their own flies. Commercially tied flies made in the region date back to before World War I, and doubtless there were more than a handful of proficient tiers prior to even that time. It is necessary to remember that in terms of materials, the old-time fly fishermen of the Smokies had access to the same materials used everywhere else in the United States. They also had access to sporting journals that revealed the latest innovations in fly fishing. Bear in mind too that nearly all of the tackle companies in those days offered extensive lines of trout flies and fly rod baits.

This was the era of mail-order catalogs made famous by Sears and Roebuck. The same hooks, threads, and dressings available to tiers in the Rockies and the Northeast could be delivered anywhere by the U.S. Postal Service. This is not to say that local tiers, including those who were well funded, did not use locally obtained furs, feathers, and other materials. However, having inspected at least three old tying kits from the 1920s that were used regionally in the Smokies, I was amazed by the number of small wax-paper envelopes containing such exotic materials as jungle cock eye plums, ostrich herl, and marabou, not to mention tinsels and bottles of glue made just for tying flies. These items were either point-of-purchase acquisitions at some well-stocked sporting goods store, or were obtained from a mail-order catalog.

Tiers commonly stay on the lookout for fly-tying components, especially if they are also hunters. Squirrels were the number-one quarry in those days, and their bushy tails have always been prized by fly tiers and lure makers. As a young man in the 1930s, Benny Craig told me that he collected discarded red plastic seal bands from packs of cigarettes to use for the midsections of his Royal Coachman dry flies. Cato Holler trekked to the Arctic to shoot a polar bear, bringing back its cap for use in creating streamers. Opossum belly fur was a favorite material of Frank Young, while Ernest Ramsey supplied himself with neck hackles from the gamecocks he kept around his home.

Matt Whittle and "Fishing" Dick Reagan were among the earliest anglers to guide the tourists who flocked to Gatlinburg around the turn of the century. It is my understanding that many of their clients were members of the country's social elite in those days. Names such as Firestone, Westinghouse, and Wrigley appeared on their rosters. Much the same occurred around Biltmore. Local guides were not only exposed to the first tackle made in those days, but also to the latest fly patterns purchased from Orvis and fabled establishments such as Abercombie and Fitch in New York City.

Doubtless their most generous clients gifted their guides with flies and on occasion their fly rods and reels. I know of a couple of extraordinarily rare Payne and Dickerson fly rods that wound up in unlikely places such as Bryson City in this manner. Suffice to say that the busiest, best-known guides such as Mark Cathey were fly-pattern savvy. Cathey may have relied on the Gray Hackle as his go-to fly, and he certainly offered it to his clients—the smart ones seized the opportunity. However, then as now, I am willing to bet that all of the old timers guided clients who "knew it all" and preferred their favorite Grizzly King. Worst of all, fishing was so good back then that they probably caught enough fish to validate their arrogance.

Of the literature we have available from 80 to 150 years ago, well over half of the patterns recommended for use in the Great Smoky Mountains are what I would term the most universally popular patterns of their era. These include the Parmachene Belle, Professor, Wickham's Fancy, Silver Doctor, Red Ibis, and Seth Green, all of which were widely used from the lakes of Maine and dashing streams of the Catskills to big waters of Canada and the flows of the Rocky Mountains. They were popular because they caught trout, and still do. They were also popular because it was rare for articles or books in those days not to tout these patterns. In a sense, they were part of the angling lexicon of the time, much the same as Compara-duns would be today.

When the old-time guides were queried about patterns, I suspect that they spoke in the language of the day so that prospective clients would not only know what to bring, but also so that they could feel confident that their guide was at least to some degree versed in the fly-fishing lingo. I believe this was especially prevalent when these guides were interviewed by writers such as Robert Mason. It was likely more a matter of communicating their knowledge of the sport to would-be clients rather than an effort to share their secrets, at least publicly. The real question is, did local tiers always mimic the better-known patterns of that era, gradually morphing patterns with a local flare, or did some of the old patterns coexist in the shadows of the nationally celebrated fly patterns?

The Tellico Nymph appears to be of genuine local origins, but the Thunderhead created by Fred Hall almost certainly did not exist until Lee Wulff's technique for creating hair wings on dry flies became common knowledge. The oldest flies that can be traced as unique to the Great Smoky Mountains date from 1880 to 1910. A good argument can be made that the Gray Hackle is the oldest, especially in the dry-fly category. I am of the opinion that soft-hackles such as the Yallarhammar and Smoky Mountain Blackbird morphed from the Leadwing Coachman.

What is clear is that following World War II there was an explosion of interest among fly tiers around the Smokies to create more patterns that produced well on these waters. Many young men, such as Fred Hall and Kirk Jenkins, returned home from the war to the region and embraced trout fishing and tying flies. They augmented their incomes by tying flies to sell locally to other fishermen and at hardware stores, and doing contract tying for companies such as South Bend and Weber. By the 1950s virtually all of the old fly patterns we find of interest today were in widespread use and beginning to attract national attention.

This is my personal theory of how it unfolded. Like all such efforts, broad brush strokes allow you to cover a lot of territory. The devil is in the details of how this fly pattern happened, or how that fly pattern came from here or there. We may never know the full story of these old flies and their daddies, but I hope if you know something that you record it in some fashion so that the history of all of this can be preserved.

CHAPTER FOUR

The Yallarhammar:
Public Enemy
Number One

A fistful of Yallarhammers, one of the most controversial fly patterns to originate in the Smokies. DON KIRK

T his book is inescapably going to court some controversy. Who created the Yallarhammar is the "mother of all controversies," at least in terms of fly patterns believed to have originated in the Great Smoky Mountains. Unless someone unearths the southern fly fishing secret book of lore, which would rank a close second behind the discovery of the Dead Sea Scrolls, I am strongly of the opinion that no one will ever identify the Yallarhammar's creator. On this there is general agreement. Yet a lot of so-called experts have peddled more than their share of crap and conjecture about this simple fly.

From a personal standpoint, I cannot recall when "Yallarhammar" was not part of my vocabulary, but then I grew up in a home where fly tying was a family business. "Yallarhammar" and "stickbait" were words that came up often in conversation at fish camps in Greenbrier and Paint Creek, TN. Although we used lots of flies that were not Yallarhammars, we always had them on hand. I've had lots of conversations with other fly fishermen of my generation, and this is pretty much as it was for everyone.

I have caught a lot of trout from the streams of the Smokies using flies that qualify as Yallarhammars. However, I probably have caught just as many trout on Tellico Nymphs, Thunderheads, Royal Coachmen, Adamses, Gray Hackles, Princes, and a few others. While the Yallarhammar in its various forms and styles is certainly an effective offering, it cannot be said that they are any more effective than many other patterns, and they certainly have no magical power as some might lead you to believe. But in our legalistic world, the Yallarhammar has garnered the reputation as "public enemy number one" because it uses feathers from the yellow-shafted flicker, a type of woodpecker. Because yellow-shafted flickers are not regarded as game or nuisance birds, there is no season or time you can kill them.

In researching the Yallarhammar, I found a number of interesting potential origins of the fly. One particularly "brilliant" source credits the Cherokee of the Qualla with introducing the Yallarhammar fly pattern to the first white folks so that the white folks could begin the task of screwing the Cherokee out of their homeland. Logic would dictate that some apparently enlightened tribal members took the time to sculpt some size 10 bone hooks. Then trial and error must have determined that the wing feathers of the yellow-shafted woodpecker made a better wet fly than those tied with the plumage of meadowlarks, goldfinches, or Connecticut warblers, all of which were equally available to the natives. One must also assume that the Cherokee actively pursued fly pattern experimentation on long winter nights in the longhouses, which naturally led to trying feathers of everything from scarlet tanagers and ruffed grouse to wood duck and ivory-billed woodpeckers. Pretty absurd, eh?

I do not contest the notion that the Cherokee may very well have created the Yallarhammar, but it certainly did not predate the arrival of Europeans, and probably it did not predate Andrew Jackson's forced removal west of the majority of the Cherokee. Armed with metal fishhooks, confined to remote corners of the mountains, and needing an efficient way to provide food likely prompted the genesis of fly tying

It is impossible to have a bad day of fishing the in the Great Smoky Mountains. JTLOCKE

among the natives. Within this scenario I can see how one might credit the Cherokee with the distinction of being the first to wrap feathers around a hook, but if they knew how to collect stickbait, why would they go to the trouble of inventing the Yallarhammar? The Yallarhammar does not seem to have been born out of necessity.

There is considerable controversy as to which of the many styles of Yallarhammar is the oldest, a question I do not believe will ever be settled, at least not until someone masters the ability to travel back in time. Early fly fishermen visiting the Smokies carried selections of wet flies, many of which were soft-hackle patterns. Theodore Gordon's high-riding dry flies were not yet around between the 1840s and 1880s when recreational fishing with flies occurred here. The locals, and this includes the Cherokee, would have had an opportunity to examine and even fish what to them must have been oddities indeed.

Most of the earliest Yallarhammar flies I have examined had plump to slender peacock herl bodies with yellow-shafted flicker wing bodies. The top wraps are naturally short, which would be consistent with what I have been told many times by old-time tiers who say they can only get five good flies per wing. When you consider that such a tying mode is completely consistent to the flies brought to the Great Smoky Mountains 150 years ago such as the Brown Hackle, Grizzly Hackle, Red

Hackle, or even the Soldier Palmer, then a good argument can be made that the first Yallarhammars had collared hackles.

Ernest Ramsey of Pigeon Forge, TN, sold these and the full-palmered Yallarhammars that some so-called experts say are the oldest of the numerous patterns now touted by today's regional tiers. These generally scraggly looking versions of the Yallarhammar are tied with the larger plums instead of the most prized wing feathers. This revelation will be contested by many, but it is consistent with what I was also told by Walter Cole, Joe Manley, and Kirk Jenkins. The shaggy versions of the Yallarhammar might be just as old as the peacock-bodied Yallarhammar, but the former was the result of tiers pushing the envelope, so to speak, by using every part of the always-tough-to-get wings and tail feathers of a yellow-shafted flicker.

Today, a number of traditional tiers on both sides of the Smokies recognize the considerable interest in the Yallarhammer, and they have taken the time to create a so-called series of Yallarhammer patterns, including a Yallarhammer dry-fly pattern. The oddest, at least in my opinion, is one called the Yallarhammer Nymph, which is nothing more than a Montana Nymph with the addition of a yellow flicker plum.

Despite the popularity of the Yallarhammer and patterns inspired by Yallarhammar, the originator of using yellow-shafted woodpecker feathers to create the Yallarhammar is unknown. Before speculating about this topic, something must be said about the woodpeckers. Several obviously ignorant "experts" refer to these birds as endangered, or presumably under federal Endangered Species Act (ESA) protection. At least one particularly "knowledgeable" source says that these birds were hunted to the brink of extinction for their feathers. For over 75 years these birds, along with scores of other so-called songbirds and similarly classified non-game birds, have enjoyed varying degrees of protection by local, state, and federal laws. However, the yellow-shafted flicker has never even remotely been threatened, nor was it ever considered for ESA listing.

Personally I have no doubt that squirrel hunters and country marksmen shot a few yellow-shafted flickers for their wing feathers. To suggest that these birds were hunted, at least with the same fervor as upland gamebirds or wildfowl, smacks of total ignorance: the old timers were shot- and powder-stingy by nature. It also shows a lack of understanding of the yellowhammer's lifestyle. While they're just as capable of machinegunlike pecking to remove insect larvae from infected trees as red-bellied woodpeckers, they spend lots of time on the ground looking for ants. On the ground, yellowhammers are vulnerable to predators ranging from foxes and bobcats to hawks and owls. Guess what these killers leave behind on the ground? Wings and tail feathers. Here's another disturbing fact: While a fortunate nine-year-old was the Methuselah of the species, four years is the average life span of these fickle flickers. In other words, virtually every woodpecker in and around the Great Smoky Mountains National Park will be dead within five years, either at the hands of predators, lightning strikes, disease, injury, or old age. If not for the miracle of these birds instinctively raising eight to twelve hatchlings on an annual basis, these birds would be extinct, ESA or no ESA. Clearly, humans are the least of the yellowhammer's worries.

Few of the tiers I have known over the years have shot yellow-shafted flickers. Most spoke of friends who found birds killed by predators or cars which they sold to them outright for a couple of dollars, or who parlayed them into half a dozen or so flies. Kirk Jenkins of Newport, TN, had a neat deal for getting more yellow-shafted flicker wings than he could use. The power company linemen in Cocke County routinely collected the wings from the birds they found inside transformer housings on telephone poles. Apparently squirrels aren't the only ones who find their way into the cozy-looking death chambers.

Woodpeckers have especially stiff tail feathers. The central tail feathers are often very pointed, with the tips tapering noticeably. Their primary feathers are most often black with white spots. Northern flickers have the most distinctive feathers of all woodpeckers because their larger feathers, such as flight feathers and tail feathers, have quills and shafts that are golden yellow (yellow shafted) or pinkish (red shafted). Easy stuff, eh?

Not really. Consider that the U.S. Air Force has a special laboratory dedicated exclusively to identifying the feathers of birds unfortunate enough to be sucked into the intakes of jet and turboprop engines. What? They need to do DNA work to see if it is a Canada goose or a speckled-bellied goose? Short of subjecting a feather to the scrutiny of a scientific expert, it is very tough to determine its species or origins with any real certainty.

Consider the following. You are fishing on the Little River where a duly authorized, uniformed National Park Service ranger approaches you. After checking to see if you have a valid fishing license and giving you a cursory pat-down for illegally creeled trout (standard procedure if you live near the park), the officer asks to inspect your fly boxes. They have a right to do so, and if they find a live grasshopper in your fly box, you have a problem. However, let's suppose the NPS servant not only doesn't like local anglers, but he's disgruntled because his wife is also way too cozy with some Cosby moonshiner. Now it gets interesting.

The ranger plucks an innocent-looking soft-hackle fly from your box. He asks if it is a Yallarhammar, which every smart fly fisherman denies since the feathers come from protected birds and cannot be used or possessed if you have poached the bird. Unfortunately, and this happens far more than you might believe, the "park pecker checker" declares it is contraband by virtue of his suspicion that you have a wicked Yallarhammar. The usual custom is that the ranger will try to confiscate the fly. Assuming they are not genuine Yallarhammar flies, you should object to the seizure.

Mind you, rangers have every right, and even an obligation, to confiscate anything illegal, including marijuana, explosives, or wild orchids found on your person while within the confines of the national park. However, while you may have flies

Backcountry streams require effort and planning to reach, but the rewards are great.
WILLIAM MCLEMORE

with a dozen other illicit materials from dodo to jungle cock feathers, the ranger's astute eyes are trained to focus on local anglers who may be poachers. If they think you have a genuine Yallarhammer, they will seize it. Here's the kicker: so long as your Yallarhammer flies were tied from legally obtained material (i.e., from a dead bird not illegally killed), you are allowed to possess them, even in the form of a fly. You might even be able to convince a ranger that it is so, but the chances are slim.

If this happens to you, the proper protocol is to ask the ranger for a receipt listing your seized property. Of course they will refuse, but once you ask, they are legally bound to comply with your request, as it is necessary to have a receipt in order to track your flies as they move through the complicated identification process. After all, if the authorities can't prove that the flies were made with illegal material, they must be returned to you in the same condition in which they were seized.

When you get home, send a letter to the superintendent of the GSMNP and to the director of the Region 4 office of the U.S. Fish and Wildlife Service, the organizations that investigate such breeches of the public peace. Make it clear to them that you are exercising your legal right to due process. This means they must allow you to inquire about the status and location of your property. I have been told that the cost of determining the identity of such snippets of plumage can exceed $5,000. Above all, don't expect from the NPS what they expect from you, which is complete, docile cooperation.

Now if the water is not muddy enough for everyone, consider this occurrence on the other side of the big pond. Noted contemporary English fly tier Oliver Edwards has developed a dry-fly pattern he has dubbed the Yellow Hammer. According to Edwards, his new pattern is deadly during the many weeks of the Yellow May emergence. "In view of my early successes with the 'Klink,' [the Klinkhamer trout fly] this all-yellow version was the logical next step for copying the stage where this very distinctive dun pops through the surface film. It was an instant success, and is very deadly during the trickle emergence of these beautiful duns. . . . I wouldn't be without it. Treat and fish it as the Klinkhamer."

Just a trout fly, eh? In a sense, the Yallarhammar encapsulates the story of fly fishing in and around the Smokies, from the origins of fly fishing in the region to modern issues about fishing regulations.

CHAPTER FIVE

Tiers in Heaven

The lower reaches of many streams in the Great Smoky Mountains are quite large. LOUIS CAHILL

The best title I could come up with for this chapter about the following Great Smoky Mountain fly tiers is "Tiers in Heaven," which is a nice way of saying they are no long eking out a hardscrabble existence on this mortal coil. Some of these men died prior to my birth, but I knew a number of them personally. My purpose for listing them along with the information about them is to make sure they are recognized for their contributions to fly fishing and fly patterns in the Great Smoky Mountains. I am the first to acknowledge that this list is incomplete, but it is the best collection of such information to date, and hopefully it inspires others to add to it.

The Great Smoky Mountains region has peculiar traditions and a history that has always fascinated a lot of people from a lot of different places, as evidenced by the rich lore of fly fishing here. I made every effort to identify all of the old-time tiers, a period I defined as the 1920s through the 1980s, and as you read this the process continues on. Doubtless I have missed a significant number of the old timers as, unlike the prestige one was afforded from owning the best coonhound in the hollow, not a lot of notoriety was attached to fly tying.

There are more similarities than differences among these men. A few, such as Kirk Jenkins, Eddy George, Cato Holler, Cap Weise, and Jim Gasque were of middle-class upbringing. Others such as Frank Young, Fred Hall, Benny Craig, Ernest Ramsey, and Claude Gossett came from more modest origins, rightly fitting the more stereotypical idea of mountain folk who grew up in the Great Depression. They all loved to fly fish, were accomplished tiers, and from my personal experiences and from the information I've gathered from others, had a passion for sharing their love and knowledge of fly fishing in the Great Smoky Mountains. I wish I could have met them all over a drink to hear their stories and observations of fly fishing for trout here over the years.

As dedicated and skilled as some of the old timers were in those days, their very existence, much less artistic fame, was known to a clannish cadre of fly fishermen who rarely shared their knowledge or the locations of their favorite haunts with others. Local anglers either knew enough about tying flies adequate for catching trout, or knew someone who did. According to Sue Lundsford of the Cosby Community, when she was a girl in the 1930s, she would run down the dominicker rooster for its neck hackles before her father went fishing in the park. Commonly called "pilgrim fowl," dominickers, or "dominiques," are America's oldest breed of chicken. Dominickers sport irregularly striped black-and-white feathers, a pattern called "barring" or sometimes "hawk coloring" in the world of poultry farming, but referred to as "grizzly" when such neck capes are offered for sale in fly shops.

Lundsford's father learned fly tying from his own father who, like his son, did not use a vise to secure hooks, much less own such a handy gadget. Hackles came from the roosters, although according to Lundsford they were quite uncooperative when it came to giving up enough neck plums needed to replenish a fly box. Peacock

For many years the spectacular fly fishing available in the Smokies was a secret. WILLIAM
MCLEMORE

herl was always plentiful as the Lundsfords, like many of their neighbors, kept free-
ranging peafowl. These birds still roam widely on the Lundsfords' farm. They roost
in trees where they are alert not only to trouble approaching on the ground, but to
the presence of chicken hawks that prey on the free-roaming chickens. Few things
are noisier that a brace of upset peacocks. If you have ever been where these birds
live, you know how common it is to find on the ground a long feather resplendent
with a generous supply of herls.

   Sewing thread, yarns, neck and saddle hackles, herl, fur for dubbing, copper
wire, quills, and of course wing feathers from crows, blackbirds, and yellow flicker
woodpeckers would have been pretty much standard fare for old-time tiers. On
two occasions during my years of chasing old tackle I came upon tying arsenals
that were considerably more sophisticated. Among other more refined mail-order
items—such as tying vise, silk thread, and head cement—were tufts of polar bear

and genuine jungle cock. One tying box even contained a 10-inch-long aluminum priest, the only such angling billy stick I found during a twenty-year stint of raiding attics and basements throughout the region.

These men are not listed in order of importance or reputation or anything other than how they came up in my notes. Again, the purpose of the work here is to share what is known about these tiers and in many cases my time spent with them between the 1970s and 1990s. From a purely historical perspective, it is the first effort to publish a list of these men and their contributions. I sincerely hope that it is the catalyst for others to contribute what they know about these fellows as well as to identify other old-time tiers.

Don Ray Howell
Pisgah Forest, NC

A preeminent Tarheel State tier, Don Ray Howell was gifted a fly-tying kit by his father who, as the result of an injury to his hand, could not tie flies. Don Ray's father was an expert fly fisherman who taught him enough about the sport that over the years Howell hooked and landed over 350 trout in the 20- to 30-inch range from the public trout waters of western North Carolina. Today his son Kevin, who owns Davidson River Outfitters, carries on the family tradition both in slaying big trout in Carolina waters, but also being a master fly fisherman and fly tier.

Don Ray Howell authored *Tying and Fishing Southern Appalachian Trout Flies* in 1999. A magazine-sized paperback, it was the first of three books that largely addressed the subject of fly patterns of the Great Smoky Mountains. Don Ray not only helped immortalize old-time patterns from his part of the world, such as the Yallarhammar and the Sheep Fly, but he also created a number of patterns of his own, such as the Hot Creek Special, Bill's Provider, Don's Pet, and Don's Woven Nymph, to name a few. He passed away at the relatively tender age of 54, which was far too early for the sort of fellow he was.

Jim Gasque
Asheville, NC

Born in 1903, Jim Gasque spent most of his formative years and his entire adult life in Asheville, NC. He was the outdoor editor for both local newspapers, the *Asheville Times* and the *Asheville Citizen*. Today Jim is best remembered as the author of *Hunting and Fishing in the Great Smokies*, which devoted eight chapters to fishing in the Great Smoky Mountains National Park and an entire chapter to the old mountaineer fly fisherman, Mark Cathey of Bryson City, NC.

Sadly, Gasque's considerable contributions to fly and lure design are largely overlooked these days. He developed the "Basstriker" (there was a lesser known "Troutstriker) in the 1930s, which was a streamer fly design that was in essence a heavy "fly rod bait." Commercial versions of the fly featured a white fabric skirt with nine fingers that undulated the bait. His prototypes had oil cloth skirts that he hand cut before developing a cutting die. He also sold Gasque "Popstrikers" at Finkelstein's Sporting Goods and Pawn Shop in Asheville (it's still located on Broad Street, but is now known as Finkelstein, Inc.). A hard bait creator as well, his Gasque Crawler later became better known as the Whopper Stopper Lizard, a name he is said to have coined. He had several patented lures that were sold under the Allen Lures name and by Lucky Bunny Bait Company. Although retired at the time of his death, Gasque still went to the office every day where he tied flies.

Eddy George
Louisville, TN

Eddy George of Louisville, TN, was born in 1922 and grew up fishing the streams in and around the Great Smoky Mountains National Park with the real old-time tiers. I first interviewed George at his lakeside home in 1987, and made a couple of visits there until the mid-1990s when he was in failing health. The creator of the famous George Nymph, George said he first tied it as a teenager in the 1930s, adding that it did not predate the Cotton Top Nymph, but was his version of it.

According to George, during his salad days spent fly fishing with long-rodders many years his senior, most of the flies he used were of English origins, and more often than not were fished using a Hilderbrant-style spinner. Even in those days most of his mentors tied their own flies, and they carried enough material with them to quickly construct a fly streamside if they found such a need.

George told me his namesake mayfly-style nymph was quite the hit. After his return from the army following World War II, George worked at the old Athletic House on Gay Street in Knoxville, a job he held throughout the 1950s. The Athletic House was the Knoxville version of Abercrombie and Fitch, and where such notables as General Neyland not only purchased jerseys and helmets for his University of Tennessee Volunteers, but also where the coach bought his bass-fishing tackle. George was the resident fly-fishing expert. He maintained a small "private stock" section where he tied in-demand patterns such as the Adams and Royal Coachman and his own patterns such as the George Nymph. Such exposure and availability contributed significantly to the George Nymph's nationally known reputation as an effective trout taker. Even today many anglers believe that the George Nymph cannot be topped as a year-round offering in the streams of the Great Smoky Mountains National Park.

Newland Saunders
Lenoir, NC

Newland Saunders from Lenoir, NC, is best remembered for the creation of the Sheep Fly, which he tied to imitate a gray fly that is commonly found around sheep. Over the fly pattern's sixty-year life span, it has been modified a few times. After learning more about the fly's etymology, it's been discovered that it actually imitates three different food groups—crane fly larvae, stickbait, and large emerging mayflies.

Newland Saunders was a genuine old-school tier who relied largely on locally available material from furs and feathers to most of the other ingredients needed to create his patterns. Aside from being an expert fly fisherman, he had a widespread reputation for helping other fly fishermen, especially young fly tiers, get traction in the sport. He tied the Sheep Fly well into his nineties. In fact, Newland passed away during the writing of this book, prompting the need to move him from one chapter to another.

Cato Holler
Marion, NC

A couple of the men noted here actually had more influence on fly fishing in the Great Smoky Mountains than they did on fly tying. However, they are part of the story I am trying to preserve, so you'll have to pardon my periodic rambling. Among Cato Holler's accomplishments as an avid, all-around fly fisherman and hunter, he authored *Adventures of a Lifetime: The Autobiography of an American Sportsman*.

Best remembered for his conservation efforts, Holler served as the founding director of Trout Unlimited. As a fly tier, he is best remembered for his innovative Infallible. He may be the only old-time Great Smoky Mountains fly tier to have trekked north to kill polar bears, whose fur he used for tying flies. Cato Oliver Holler was ninety-seven years old when he died on May 22, 2001, at his home.

Ernest Ramsey
Pigeon Forge, TN

As best as I can determine, there was but one local builder of bamboo rods in the 1940s among the now-passed-on old timers: Ernest Ramsey, located in Pigeon Forge. The Ramsey Rods, built completely from scratch, lacked the exquisite craftsmanship of those from the shops in the East, but they exhibited a fine feel and were affordable. Those that remain today are treasured by their owners.

I met Ernest Ramsey around 1973. At that time he had long stopped making split-cane bamboo rods, but he still tied flies. In his youth Ramsey often made himself available as a guide, although according to him, it was anything but steady work

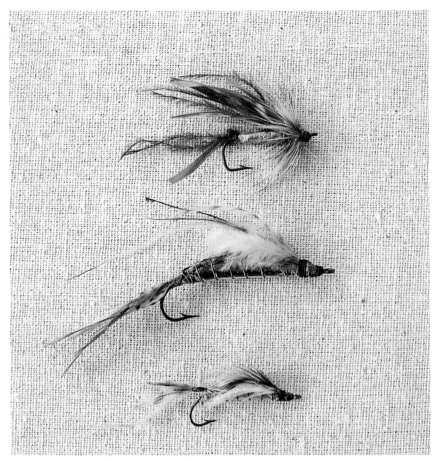

Louis Rhead flies. The connection between Louis Rhead and Horace Kephart (see the next page) is a discovery I made while researching this book. DAVID BUSH

in those days. When I visited his living room—from which he sold flies—Ramsey had about a dozen different pattern selections, the most exotic being a single dun wing Royal Coachman. The flies were dirt cheap in 1970, $3 a dozen, and if you looked closely at them you might easily have guessed they were a bit overpriced. However, they caught trout—and lots of them—on a consistent basis. They were also tough as nails, taking more abuse than any fly you could order from Vermont in those days. He always offered us a sip from a fruit jar whenever we made a stop by his home on Middle Creek. Smooth, no; but certainly warming.

Ramsey's fly-tying business was more of a sideline, as he was perhaps Sevier County's best-known trainer and fighter of gamecocks. To say he had a never-ending supply of fresh hackles would be quite an understatement. Ramsey showed me his rod-making gear once and offered to sell it to me along with a big armload of Tonkin bamboo in the raw. I was perhaps twenty years old then and way too smart to waste money on those dust-encrusted contraptions.

Along with a couple of varieties of Yallarhammar, Crow, Tellico, Royal Coachman, Adams and other patterns (nothing tied with a hook smaller than a size 14), Ramsey also had his favorite, which he said had been shown to him by his father who also regarded the pattern as his fly of choice. He called it the Ramsey Fly, but I would call it a Brown Hackle dry. Quite unsophisticated, this monotone pattern works well on park waters. I asked the old man where in the park his folks lived, to which he said his daddy's daddy was from "up" near the cascades of the Middle Prong of the Little Pigeon River. When queried if the creek there was his family's namesake, his only response was, "that's what I've heard tell all my life." He was more interested in fighting chickens than the details of family history.

Horace Kephart
Bryson City, NC

To the best of my knowledge Horace Kephart never tied a single fly that he fished in the Great Smoky Mountains. He is listed here solely for his historical connection to the overall story. A few have written incorrectly that Kephart did not fly fish, but he was actually an avid fly fisherman during his long stint in the Deep Creek area of the Smokies. I have personally inspected his fly wallet, which is held in the archives at Western Carolina University. Although until then unidentified, I recognized several of the flies in the wallet. My long background in dealing with antique fishing tackle alerted me to the fact that these flies were the product of Louis Rhead, a well-known early-twentieth-century fly tier and illustrative artist.

Further investigation unearthed a letter from Louis Rhead to Horace Kephart talking about the very flies still in the wallet. Kephart's inclusion here is largely based on his writings about fishing in the Great Smoky Mountains, and the Rhead correspondence further demonstrates that fishing in the area has long had the attention of fly fishermen across the United States. Rhead's most famous and celebrated work is *American Trout-Stream Insects* (1916). At the time of its publication, the book was one of the first and most comprehensive studies of stream entomology ever published in America.

Paul Schullery in *American Fly Fishing—A History* (1987) says this about Rhead: "Louis Rhead was one of the most creative, fresh-thinking, and stimulating of American fly-fishing writers, a man of extraordinary gifts."

Jack Cabe
Highlands, NC

Jack Cabe, developer of the Cabe's Hopper, was the proprietor of Mainstream Out-fitters in Highlands, NC. Cabe was born in Highlands on October 10, 1942, and grew up there like the six generations of his family before him. He and and his wife Joan, also a seventh-generation Highlander, began dating in high school. After Cabe finished his degree at Western Carolina University, they were married in October 1963 and had two children, Patricia and Geoffrey. The Cabes were a fishing family. Pat and Geoff also became accomplished fly fishers. And Joan continues to instruct women in fly fishing.

On one fly-fishing trip to the Rockies, Cabe fished pattern called a Michigan Hopper. He saw the potential for a Smoky Mountain attractor in that fly, and brought it back to western North Carolina. He based his Cabe's Hopper on it, which he created out of the material he had on hand. He developed a few other patterns that bear his name and are popular among local fly fishermen.

Kirk Jenkins
Newport, TN

Kirk Jenkins is my favorite among the old-time tiers. Early on, this fly-tying guru took me under his wing. Although he was not a card-carrying native of Cocke County, TN, the moonshine capital of the planet, Kirk grew up there and the Smoky Mountains were always his home. When I met Kirk he was a supervisor at American Enka, where I was employed in those days. He was soft-spoken and articulate, and at the time I did not recognize his artistic talents as a photographer and painter, which came to be widely known later.

Kirk tied great trout-catching flies. His Little River Ants, Yallarhammars, Smoky Mountain Forky Tail Nymphs, and others were $4 a dozen, which even then was a steal. He always included a couple of other fly patterns in my orders that he wanted me to test for him. Years later, when I thanked Kirk for his patience and goodwill, he confided that he knew I was "trouble," and that I was less likely to do something really outrageous that would result in jail time if I was out on a trout stream. Considering the activities that I managed to combine with trout fishing, he was probably right. To seal my fate, he gave me his old Herter's vise to help occupy my time when I was not buns deep in a creek, but still able to steer myself in the direction of mischief.

A decorated World War II veteran, Kirk's mastery of feather, hook, and tread exceeded the quality and durability of other locally available flies. He was one of a few tiers around then who had some experience selling work to nationally recog-nized tackle makers. In this case it was Weber, a company that appears to have had some strong eastern Tennessee contacts, as at the same time they bought flies tied by Eddy George. According to Kirk, he got pretty fast at tying Weber's Humbug Fly

Plunge pools like this often harbor dozens of rainbow and brook trout. WILLIAM MCLEMORE

Rod Floaters and their Parmachene Bass Flies, but he regarded their deer-hair flies, such as their popular Whiskerbug and Henshall Floating Lure, as too time consuming to create. Jenkins also sold his own patterns to Weber that are not found in the catalogs, but most likely were sold around the park where Weber sales representatives went door-to-door at hardware and country stores.

Benny Joe Craig
Waynesville, NC

Benny Joe Craig of Waynesville, NC, is the uncontested old-time master fly tier of the Smokies. At least a second-generation trout fishing expert and master fly tier, Craig not only originated many of the fly patterns we use today, but he also trained or influenced virtually everyone now tying flies in western North Carolina. He learned to tie flies by watching my father. According to Craig there were farms in a three-county area in those days where he chased down roosters to pick a few choice neck hackles.

"As a young fly tier," said Craig, "my friends and I were exceptionally fond of floating Royal Coachman dries at these streams. For our home-tied Royal Coachman flies we used the bright red plastic band used to seal packs of Lucky Strike cigarettes. Early on Saturday mornings, we would go to downtown Waynesville to patrol the streets for discarded plastic bands for making these flies."

Craig's all-time favorite fly pattern was the Adams. Of course, he carried these in a wide assortment of sizes and varieties, in-cluding the Adams Parachute and Adams Wulff, as well as the Black Adams and the Adams Vari-ant. In addition, Craig also varied the body of the Adams he fished, using dark bodies in late winter and spring and lighter bodies in sum-mer. Similarly, he switched from a dark brown hackle in winter and spring to a grizzly hackle in summer.

Craig preferred to keep his fly pattern selection ultrasimple. He had several recom-mendations he knew would consistently produce trout in these waters at certain times of the year, including the well-known Thunderhead and the Chocolate Thunder-

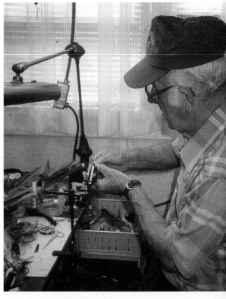

Benny Joe Craig JIM CASADA

head, which in his opinion differ little from an Adams Wulff. He also created the Elk Wing Hopper, which features flanks dressed with a speckled feather from a bronze-colored domestic turkey. He also spoke highly of the Orange Palmer. He believed it dates to at least the 1930s and originated in Haywood County, NC.

According to Craig, nothing tops the old-fashioned Stickbait Nymph for the chore of catching trout. He tied his from special latex material that perfectly matches the dingy, yellowish-white color of these highly sought-after trout foods. But the longtime angler was quick to point out that nothing was better than the real thing—soft, pulpy stickbait.

Craig shared his knowledge of many old fly patterns with me, including the rarely seen (these days, anyway) Wasp Nymph and the Forked Tail Pale Watery Dun. The latter fly has large mallard wings and a large, forked tail that enables it to ride high in the water. Lastly, he spoke of tying a lot of Green Inchworm patterns as well as his own Sourwood Worm that he created at the request of his son, Kevin.

Charles C. Messer
Haywood County, NC

One of the long-gone tiers of the old, post–World War II days, Charles C. Messer was one of the first fly fishermen in the region to make a concerted effort to record information about flies. About the shadow boxes used to display the flies he called "Old Fly Patterns of the Appalachians," he said: "My brother and I have used these patterns for sixty-five years and they will still take fish. The purpose of this display is to keep and preserve the Appalachian patterns lest they be lost." Patterns found in the display are: Gray Hackle, Brown Hackle, Gray Peacock, Forked Tail, Nantahala Special, Male Adams, Orange Mayfly, Yellow Mayfly, Green Stone, and Yellow Stone. Ironically, Charley's Whooper, one of the patterns he originated, is not found in the display cases you can still buy online.

Fred Hall
Bryson City, NC

Fred Hall and his spouse, Allene, were the Great Smoky Mountains' version of Harry and Elsie Darbee, the well-known fly-tying team who ran their business from their home in Livingston Manor, a short distance away from the Willowemoc Creek, a feeder stream of the Beaverkill River in New York. One of the best-known old-time tiers, Hall worked from his home in Bryson City, NC. His flies, and particularly his dry flies, were renowned for their symmetry, sparseness, and great attention to detail. I was introduced to Hall in the late 1970s by Wendell Crisp, who sold Hall's flies from an old-fashioned glass case in his hole-in-the-wall store located in the heart of Bryson City. Crisp was an excitable fellow with a dual passion for Hall's well-tied fly patterns (as well as those of other local tiers such as Frank Young) and his never-ceasing vendetta against the National Park Service, which had not only forcibly removed his family from their home in the middle of the night on Hazel Creek, but, according to Crisp, also torched their dwelling. This was not unusual at the time, as many families were forcibly removed from their homes by the Tennessee Valley Authority (TVA) after that body condemned their land for the construction of Fontana Dam in the early 1940s. It was not uncommon for families to be roused from bed in the middle of the neight, kicked out of their homes, and made to watch as their homes were burned to the ground.

Wounded in combat during World War II, Fred Hall returned to his Appalachian home, pawned his shotgun for $50, and purchased supplies to tie flies. He never finished high school and he never set foot on a college campus. Fred was at an advanced age when I met him, but still quite agile behind his tying vise, as was his wife. The two eked out a decent living tying flies, which in those days was quite an accomplishment considering that flies were imported from India by the boxcar load. The Thunderhead, the Halls' Wulff-style Adams Variant christened in honor of Thunderhead Mountain—which separates Bryson City from Cade Cove in Tennessee—was the couple's most prominent fly pattern. Fred's Adams Variant was also popular, although his wife tied most of these patterns; the same is true of the less well-known Caddisbuck.

Among the old-time tiers of the region Hall may have been the most business savvy. By consistently creating and selling outstanding dry and wet flies, he and his wife grew their largely local business to a nationally established one with a mail-order customer base. Like others, Fred learned his fly-tying skills at a young age from the considerable pool of fly fishermen in the Bryson City area. He is believed to be the first tier in the vicinity of the Great Smoky Mountains to incorporate the kilp-tail style, which adds hair wings to patterns that were already well-established locally such as the Adams, which he says dates to the 1940s. After his death, his wife continued the family fly-tying business until her death. I can empathize with the Halls—I know firsthand how tough it is to make a living at a vise, as I grew up tying flies just about every evening and weekend for the family business during the 1950s and 1960s.

L. J. DeCuir
Knoxville, TN

L. J. DeCuir was a stage-lighting specialist by profession at the University of Tennessee, but one of his passions was fly fishing and tying flies. In 2000, Menasha Ridge Press of Birmingham, AL, published his book, *Southeastern Flies*, the first book devoted exclusively to trout flies used on southern freestone streams and tailwater coldwater fisheries. At the time I was Menasha Ridge's longest-tenured fishing book author and was asked to review the manuscript. I found it to be concise and comprehensive, and I gave it a thumbs-up.

A detailed, well-illustrated, and well-written resource, DeCuir's book is sadly out of print at this writing. Unfortunately for all, his untimely death in 2003 robbed the southern fly-fishing community of one of its true treasures. In his book, DeCuir devotes an entire section to origins of the flies of the Great Smoky Mountains. Of particular interest is DeCuir's recognition of a series of flies by Pat Proffitt, an east Tennessee–based tier who originated such locally popular patterns as Pat's Nymph. DeCuir also befriended Bobby Shults, who at the time time ran the Smoky Mountain Angler in Gatlinburg. Shults's two best-known original patterns, the Sunshine Fly and the Buckwheat Fly, are named after dogs owned by his daughter and son-in-law.

Frank Young
Bryson City, NC

Lee Wulff's hair-wing flies had quite an impact on fly tying in and around the Smokies. Sturdier than hackled collars or hackled collars with feather wings, Wulff-style hair wings possess other characteristics that make them exceedingly popular on park waters. They have superior buoyancy and the snow-white wings serve as mini-flags atop the fly that make it easier to see in these waters than other, more traditional patterns. As with nearly everything else that found its way into the Southern

Highlands, the knowledge needed to create Wulff-style hair-wing flies was quickly co-opted by the fly tiers and fishermen of the region. As inevitably happens among mountain folk, the next step was adapting the new technology in a way that was less expensive and relied on locally available materials.

Frank Young of Bryson City was a personification of the Scots-Irish stock that established their presence in the region. While I was visiting with Wendell Crisp in Bryson City, Young entered Crisp's store where he and I were introduced—this was the only time I ever had a chance to talk to him. Our conversation centered on trout fishing in the Smokies, and inevitably the subject of flies came up. At Crisp's prompting Young pulled out a small, sectioned fly box made of once-clear plastic that had acquired an opaque patina with time that masked its contents.

Young plucked out a pair of size 10 Thunderheads identical in most aspects to the flies in Crisp's case. The hair wings, however, were bushier and a bit longer than

The well-oxygenated waters of the Great Smoky Mountains are classic examples of stonefly habitats. WILLIAM MCLEMORE

the kip-tail wings used on other Wulff-style dry flies. The fur was considerably smaller in diameter than kip tail. Further examination of the fly box revealed other flies such as a Royal Coachman and March Brown with these unorthodox hair wings, which Young explained to me were from the belly fur of a possum. In true mountain tradition, it was a cost-cutting maneuver as well as a practical choice on his part, which was apparently a matter of principle since Young owned expensive cane fly rods created by makers such as Hardy and F. E. Thomas and understood fine fishing tackle. Instead, he chose to be self-sufficient in the creation of his personal flies by using locally available possum fur and other materials.

This is not to say that in the early 1960s kip tails were not a bit pricey. My dad bought them at $1.50 to $2 a gross, which may not sound like a lot these days, but in those days the minimum wage was $1.15 and a buck got you over four gallons of gasoline. It is perhaps a bit of a stretch to include Frank Young among the old-time tier elites, but his all-hillbilly special, the possum hair wing version of the Thunderhead, is certainly worthy of note.

As did many fly fishermen of his era, Frank used long, 15- to 18-foot monofilament, but he preferred tapered leaders, which were only available commercially as long as 10–12 feet in those days. He kept a box full of spools of various monofilament sizes made by various companies from which he crafted his own 18-foot-plus-long tapered leaders. Before hitting a creek with these homemade leaders, he eliminated any stiffness in the connecting sections by baking them in the oven at 180 degrees.

Marty Maxwell
Robbinsville, NC

Marty Maxwell grew up in Graham County in the southwestern corner of North Carolina, where his grandfather taught him the local methods for catching trout. He fished these trout streams for over fifty years, and tied fly patterns for almost as long. A consummate all-around outdoorsman, he was a student of Horace Kephart, the man known as the "Dean of American Campers." Years ago Maxwell wrote his thesis for a master's degree in history at Wake Forest University on Horace Kephart. He was one of the most revered fly tiers in western North Carolina, with the MarMax Hopper being one of his best-known originals.

George "Cap" Weise
Lenior, NC

Cap Weise was the longtime headmaster at the Patterson School for Boys in Lenior City in the 1930s, and he was also a dry-fly fishing purist until he was introduced to the Sheep Fly by its originator, Newland Saunders, a fellow fly fisherman and tier from his hometown. Weise in turn passed on his passion for fishing the Sheep Fly to Don Howell, who is largely responsible for making the pattern as well known as it is today. Howell termed the Sheep Fly the "Cadillac of all nymphs."

Cap was "country" to the core. He relished venison in all forms, including raccoon or "Hoover pigs" as they were known during the Great Depression, which he served to the students of his school. He was a competitive fly fisherman to his last days, according to those who fished with him, and you fished behind Cap, as it was virtually impossible to catch up to and pass him on a stream.

Wiley Oakley
Gatlinburg, TN

In the early 1900s, trout fishermen in Knoxville, Nashville, and other cities on both sides of the mountains sought out Wiley Oakley, a local guide whose knowledge of the Smokies has never been surpassed. Known as the "Roaming Man" due to his frequent long trips into the remote recesses of the Great Smoky Mountains, Wiley was not what many expected from guides. His knowledge extended beyond where to find the best fishing for trout. He knew the plants, the trees, and seemingly every blade of grass. He even knew secret places in the mountains to hide and wait out storms or sudden changes in weather. As his guide reputation grew, he soon found himself conducting governors, congressmen, businessmen, and celebrities from all parts of the nation into the forbidding mountains to fish. The stories they brought back to their homes encouraged others to travel to the region to meet Wiley Oakley. Letters poured into his little Gatlinburg shop from across the nation. They ranged from people he had guided on tours thanking him to writers wanting to meet and record the wealth of knowledge he had gained throughout his life in the region.

When the government began the process of establishing the Smoky Mountains as a national park, scientists from Knoxville and the Smithsonian Institution who hired Wiley Oakley as a guide were simply astounded at his ability to show them numerous plants, flora, and ferns never before catalogued in America. His knowledge of every possible nook and cranny in the mountain folds was priceless to them and he soon became a major consultant during the park's formation. Surveyors called on him repeatedly to help establish park boundaries.

Prior to her passing some years ago, Wiley Oakley's daughter Lucinda Ogle spoke with me one afternoon in the 1970s when she was ninety-three years old. She told me that her father was a skilled fly fisherman, but he preferred taking her "trout choking." According to Lucinda, this was the practice of tying a small pebble to a string and dangling it into a pool. The trout would take the pebble as it was bounced along the bottom. The trick then was to allow the trout enough time to ingest the pebble, thus allowing you to pluck the trout from its watery home.

Others

By discussing the gentlemen that I have in this chapter, I've made the first effort at recording the past as it is known today. There are others such as Frank Coffey, an old steam locomotive engineer from Maggie Valley, NC, who later in life helped restore the engines still in use today by the Tweetsie Railroad. He is best remembered for devising the locally popular Coffey Stonefly Nymph out of scrap material from the Waynesville Dayco plant. There is also Claude Gossett, another western North Carolina tier who was a fishing buddy of Mark Cathey. Gossett is believed to have created the Herby-Werby pattern. Another was Harry Ijams, Knoxville's earliest ornithologist, whose fly-tying kit was recently found in that city. It contained, among other things, monkey fur, which noted fly tier Walter Babb of Sweetwater, TN, tied into Ijams's patterns to sell at auction by Trout Unlimited.

I wish I knew more about Richard Columbus "Fishing Dick" Reagan of Gatlinburg (1902–1959), whose name came up often in conversations with the old timers. He has been suggested as the creator of the Yallarhammar. Like most of the old tiers, he never used a vise to secure hooks, but did it all by hand from feathers and fur he personally collected, often from roadkill. According to Walter Cole and Joe Manley, Reagan and his fishing pal, Wiley Oakley, were not only inseparable friends but two of the best fly fishermen in that mountain community. Oakley, who has been called the "Will Rogers of the Smokies" for his sense of humor, was the more colorful and self-promoting of the duo.

A couple of other old-time tiers who slipped away before I could snare them are Freddie Moses of Knoxville and G. Neil Daniels of Greensboro, NC, both of whom were lawyers. Moses coauthored *Charley Dickey & Fred Moses Trout Fishing.* I knew Charley Dickey, a mentor of mine, well. I was around Freddie Moses several times, but in those days I was more interested in his stories about running the football for General Neyland's University of Tennessee Volunteers than his fly tying. According to "Chum," as many of us referred to Charley, Freddie Moses modified the old Woodruff pattern to have kip-tail, hair-style wings, and he refined other patterns as well to be more effective on park waters. Some great stories just slip away unrecorded.

G. Neil was a noted attorney from Greensboro who is credited with the creation of the G. Neil Fly, a dandy wet-fly pattern said to have evolved from a native Canadian fly Neil received in the 1930s. By the time I made the effort to track him down he had passed away, and I learned that he had been a lifetime bachelor with no heirs I could locate.

CHAPTER SIX

Contemporary Tiers of the Great Smoky Mountains

Brown trout of this size are quite common in the Smokies. LOUIS CAHILL

The region surrounding the Great Smoky Mountains is abuzz with talented trout-fly tiers. Some work hard to faithfully produce traditional patterns, while others work to produce more innovative fly patterns. The following is my attempt to record those who I regard as the best and most noteworthy. Of course it does not include everyone, and in some cases I am sure omissions that I made will be pointed out.

These tiers fall (more or less) into two categories. One is what I would term the tiers of traditional patterns. The other group focuses more on reinvention, especially when it comes to using the latest approaches to fly design and materials. This is not to say that the traditional tiers are "stuck" in the past in any way. However, they clearly share a keen interest in helping preserve the story of fly fishing in the Great Smoky Mountains.

A number of these fellows tie commercially, which means that they will sell you flies. Some of them have an online presence and others own or work at fly shops. A few still operate out of their garages, and a good many of these tiers also augment their income by guiding on local waters. A few simply love fly fishing and have discovered that tying flies greatly enhances their pursuit of this passion.

I've made considerable effort to locate tiers around the Great Smoky Mountains. The goal was to be as inclusive as possible, and to get this information recorded. This is just a starting point, not the final word. For now though, this is what I have to share. For the most part I have spent a little time with all of these fellows, and I genuinely like them all. In fact, I do not recall ever meeting a fellow fly fisherman who had a passion for the sport or the Great Smoky Mountains that I did not immediately feel a comfortable level of kinsmanship.

Byron Begley
Townsend, TN

A native of Kentucky, Byron Begley opened up Little River Outfitters in the 1990s, evolving it into what some regard as the premier fly shop in the Southern Appalachians. Despite tying flies since he was eleven years old, Byron is quite modest about his prowess at the vise, deferring the term "master tier" to the many local celebrity tiers who demonstrate their skills at his shop in Townsend. Byron regularly fishes traditional Great Smoky Mountains fly patterns such as the Tellico Nymph and the Adams—because according to him "they catch fish"—and he is deeply committed to the preservation and continuance of this aspect of the sport. For more info visit www.littleriveroutfitters.com.

Joel Dean
Nolensville, TN

Joel Dean is a Nashville-based fly tier who burst on the scene with the establishment of his Web-based business, Tennessee Traditional Flies. His tying efforts and photography helped make this book possible. A native of Columbus, OH, Dean has been tying since the early 1970s, and commercially for three years. He is also active in the Middle Tennessee FFF and teaches aquatic entomology and fly-fishing classes throughout the region.

Dean is of particular interest to me in that he is dedicated to the preservation and creation of traditional southern trout flies tied from materials used by the old timers. I told him on more than one occasion that he is the person who should be writing this book instead of me. For more information on his flies, or to purchase some from him, visit www.tennesseetraditionalflies.com. The website is chock-full of information on southern trout flies as well as loads of useful information on fly fishing Joel's favorite waters for trout.

Roger Lowe
Waynesville, NC

Roger Lowe grew up fishing the streams in and around the Great Smoky Mountains. No one has done more to preserve the legacy of the traditional fly patterns of the area. His book, *Roger Lowe's Fly Pattern Guide to the Great Smoky Mountains*, is a gorgeous, full-color 11" x 9" title that is found in the library of every southern fly tier. An extraordinarily talented tier, Lowe, as a young man in the 1970s, was tutored by a bevy of old timers such as Frank Coffey and Benny Joe Craig. They schooled him on traditional patterns and styles, which might very well have been lost if Roger had not invested the effort in learning them. We owe him a great debt for his foresight and diligence. Roger also has a DVD on fly tying, showing step by step how he ties some of those same patterns. He was featured on and tied the flies for the poster "Traditional Trout Flies of the Southern Appalachians," published by the Wildlife Commission.

Roger writes a column, "Featured Fly of the Month" in every issue of *Southern Trout Magazine*. He also is a much-sought-after guide on a wide variety of waters in western North Carolina and east Tennessee. He can be contacted at rogerlowe26 @gmail.com or (828) 400-7415.

Walter Babb
Sweetwater, TN

Walter Babb grew up in east Tennessee and has been fly fishing in the mountains since he was a child. He has taught fly tying and beginner fly-fishing classes at Little River Outfitters in Townsend for years. He specializes in tying mountain patterns and readily shares his experience and knowledge about fishing these rivers with the patterns that he has perfected. Since retiring, Walter has also become a professional bamboo rod maker.

Among Walter's virtues is his unassuming nature and big smile. It is not uncommon for him to introduce himself as the brother of James Babb, editor of *Gray's Sporting Journal*. If there is a dean of Great Smoky Mountains fly tying, then I can think of no one other than Walter Babb.

Kevin Howell
Pisgah Forest, NC

Growing up as the son of a nationally known fly tier and fisherman, Kevin returned to the area after college and took a teaching job so that he could have his summers free to fish. In 1997 Kevin became the manager of Davidson River Outfitters. He was also helping his father, Don Ray Howell, run Dwight and Don's Custom Tackle. After his father passed away in 1998, Kevin took over the operation of Dwight and Don's but remained at Davidson River Outfitters. Kevin has also put his vast knowledge of the sport into developing a fly-fishing school curriculum, and is also a Federation of Fly Fishers Certified Casting Instructor. Kevin is a nationally known fly tier and is currently the Southeast Ambassador for Sage Rods and a signature fly designer for Umpqua Feather Merchants. Several of his original patterns have been published in various magazines and are produced by national tying companies.

Jim Ellison
Morristown, TN

A lifelong fly fisherman with a love for catching trout in the Great Smoky Mountains, Jim Ellison is a talented and innovative tier who befriended me in the 1970s. I lived in Morristown when he was the city engineer there, and we often fished together, especially for smallmouth bass on the nearby Nolichucky River. Besides being a fly tier of some renown, Ellison is also a master rod builder. His Greenbrier series of elk wing caddis-style flies were prominently featured in my earlier guidebook to fly fishing the national park. I wish I had a dollar for every one of those flies that he tied for me over the years.

Low water in summer can make fly fishing more challenging. WILLIAM MCLEMORE

Bill Everhardt
Caldwell County, NC

A native of Caldwell County, NC, Bill Everhardt has garnered regional as well as state notoriety over the years by collecting and preserving the historical patterns of the area's trout fishermen stretching back over the generations, many of whom were mentors to Bill as well as personal friends. Bill has carefully maintained their contributions to the art of imitative fly tying. Through articles, museum exhibitions, and personal instruction, he continues to pass down the knowledge and expertise to younger enthusiasts. Cap Weise, who was discussed in chapter 5, was a personal friend of Everhardt's and was his first fly-tying instructor.

Roger Caylor
Milton, Florida

Roger Caylor is a native of Boone, NC. He fished the streams there and in the Great Smoky Mountains all of his life, but he has since retired with this wife to Florida so they can be closer to their grandchildren. A master fly tier with over four decades of experience, Roger launched launched Caylor Custom Flies in 1991. His small fly-tying company specializes in fly patterns that imitate aquatic insects indigeneous to the southern Appalachian Mountains, as well as traditional Smoky Mountain "fly hooks." In addition, his company also ties the more commonly fished flies that are popular with fly fishers on trout streams across the United States. Whenever possible Roger uses old-time ingredients for his traditional southern flies, although he does confess to occasionally substituting foam in some patterns, especially hoppers and ants. For more information visit www.caylorcustomflies.com.

Ray Ball
Gatlinburg, TN

Ray Ball, a consummate outdoorsman, is one of the true treasures of fly fishing in the Great Smoky Mountains. If there is anything that he likes better than trekking the headwaters of streams in the national park for speckled trout, it is running his beloved Walkers after "b'ar" and coons. He is a master storyteller who can keep you entertained all day. As a fly tier, Ray is frequently asked to show his stuff at venues around the Southeast. He is well versed in the creation of just about any obscure traditional Great Smoky Mountains fly pattern, although from a personal standpoint, 90 percent of his fishing in the national park is done with a variety of different-colored parachute-style dry flies.

Ray lost several fingers when he was a lad in a mishap with some dynamite blasting caps that he found stored away in his grandfather's basement. In typical "make it work" east Tennessee mountaineer fashion, Ball says he turned this obvious disadvantage to his favor by developing a number of unique fly-tying techniques, such as being among the first to apply foam for fly bodies and refine parachute wings on existing trout fly patterns that are already popular in the region.

Anthony Hipps
Lexington, NC

Anthony Hipps is a professional fly-tying artist, instructor, and speaker who has been tying flies for more than twenty years. Anthony's currently working on fleshing out the manuscript for a book on tying warmwater flies. He is also active with the Federation of Fly Fishers Southeastern Council, serving on the board of directors and as the council's Fly Tying Chairman for the past several years. He is best known for his Hipps's Soft-Foam Popper and Hipps's HellCraw Nymph, which work well on trout and smallmouth bass.

Tyler Legg
Charlotte, NC

Tyler Legg grew up fishing the trout streams of western North Carolina. Shortly after discovering fly fishing, he was introduced to fly tying. Tyler specializes in tying semi-realistic patterns, along with his popular Extended Body Inchworm and Vinyl Rib Stone. Until recently Tyler kept himself sane when not on the river by writing about fly fishing in North Carolina at his blog, Tar Heel Fly Fishing. He is currently pursuing a serious interest in music along with his passion for fly fishing and tying flies.

Rex Wilson
Candler, NC

Rex Wilson has fished in the mountains of the western region of North Carolina for most of his seventy-two years. He specializes in tying Smoky Mountain patterns and teaches fly tying and fly fishing at the Pisgah Center for Wildlife Education. He is also involved with Casting for Recovery. Rex is a member of FFF and is regularly featured tying flies at their southeastern conclaves. Besides specializing in keeping the traditional patterns of the Great Smoky Mountains alive, Rex is also an innovative tier who creates realistic fly patterns that are so lifelike you cannot help but wonder if they will crawl free from your fly box.

Ron Gaddy
Waynesville, NC

Ron Gaddy comes from Waynesville, NC, and started fishing in the Great Smoky Mountains at an early age. He grew up fishing the Cataloochee, the East and West Forks of the Pigeon River, the Little East Fork of the Pigeon River, the Nantahala River, and Jonathan Creek. Ron left North Carolina at age twenty-four for a career with the Department of Defense at Charleston, SC, and Norfolk, VA. After retiring from the DOD in 2009 he returned to Waynesville to be close to all the great trout fishing. Since retirement, Ron has consistently fished in the Smoky Mountains for trout. When not fishing, Ron ties flies and builds fly rods. His San Ron Worm, which utilizes the rubbery legs of a children's toy he purchases in quantities from dollar stores in Tennessee and North Carolina, is one of the most successful trout catchers ever to come out of the Smokies. Using the hot pink-colored appendages to the toy, Gaddy has hit upon a pattern that may be the best ever for catching trout from these waters under almost any condition.

Steve Yates
Hillbilly Hollow, NC

Steve is a North Carolina native who grew up with a love for all things outdoors. He is an avid camper, hiker, backpacker, rock climber, and bird-watcher, and is a self-taught lover of identifying the local flora and fauna. Steve specializes in trout fishing and tying flies for catching trout in the Southern Appalachians. He can often be found camping and fishing on one of his favorite streams in the Great Smoky Mountains National Park, or on one of the region's freestones or tailwaters. He enjoys tying and fishing old historic patterns of the region and is well versed in their history, as well the rich history of the southern Appalachian region that he has fished for almost forty years. Steve enjoys working with and teaching new fly fishermen and tiers the craft through numerous programs sponsored by the North Carolina Wildlife Commission and his local parks and recreation board. Steve writes for several regional newsletters and enjoys doing numerous fly-tying demonstrations for local events and charities such as Troutfest, WNC Expo, Easter Seals, Wounded Warriors, TU, FFF, and Casting for Recovery. Visit him at a show to inquire about any events at which you might like to have him do a guest appearance.

Kevin Howell

Jeff Wilkins
Summerfield, NC

Jeff Wilkins's first memory of fishing with his father is of catching a 10-inch rainbow as a young boy. Fishing has been something he has enjoyed for four decades, and he's been an avid fly fisherman for the past twenty-four years. He does this with the support and encouragement of his wife Kathy and his sons Ben and Josh. While attending the University of North Carolina at Greensboro he guided trips and tied flies on the side. Since that time, he has been involved in four retail fly-fishing operations, and has traveled both locally and to different areas of the country fly fishing, guiding, tying, and teaching.

Jeff is a Federation of Fly Fishers Certified Casting Instructor, and teaches the fly-fishing and fly-tying curriculums at both the University of North Carolina at Greensboro and Guilford Technical Community College. Fly tying is his passion. His specializes in flies, especially emergers and nymphs, for tough, selective trout. Some of his favorite patterns are published, most recently in *Trout Flies of the East* by Ted Leeson and Jim Schollmeyer. He also tied the flies for the commemorative print of Charles Kuralt, painted by Bob Timberlake, entitled *Kuralt at White's Creek*.

Bo Cash
Morganton, NC

Bo Cash was born in Morganton and still lives a short distance away, on top of a wooded ridge looking out at Table Rock Mountain. For almost three decades Bo taught biology, ecology, and general science at schools in Cleveland and Burke Counties. Fly fishing in and around the Great Smoky Mountains has been his passion from a young age. Bo cast his first fly rod when he eight years old, then shortly thereafter took up fly tying and rod building before he finally opened a fly shop he

Walter Babb

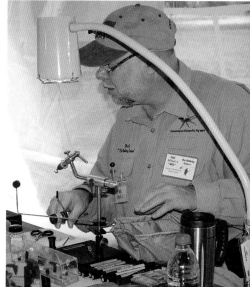

Bill Boyd Jr.

still operates, Table Rock Angler. He has been the vice president and president of his local Trout Unlimited chapter, Table Rock TU, and he remains on the chapter's board of directors. He has served as treasurer and vice chairman of the NC Trout Unlimited council, and was the associate editor of the state TU newspaper. Well versed in the traditional flies of the region, he identifies the Elk Hair Caddis as his favorite pattern followed by his own variation of a Gold-Ribbed Hare's Ear Nymph.

Oliver "Ollie" Smith
Foscoe, NC

Regarded by many as one of the most colorful modern fly tiers hailing from the Tarheel State, Oliver "Ollie" Smith was born in Charlotte in 1963. He started fishing soon thereafter, but in 1982 a life-changing event occurred: he was bitten by the fly-fishing bug as soon as he started college at Appalachian State.

In 1995 he became part-owner of Foscoe Fishing Company, the Orvis store located between Boone and Banner Elk. Then in 2001 he realized, although he was the lead guide for Foscoe, that his heart was in guiding, not retail. Since that time, he has devoted his efforts to guiding and tying flies. His favorite dry fly, although pretty much just a summer to early-fall fly, is a beetle pattern, followed by a Zebra Midge

Dave Hise
Hickory, NC

Dave Hise began his passion for fly tying in Michigan where he worked for Dick Pobst, a local fly shop owner, author of several classic guides to trout stream insects, and the creator of the Pobst Nympho, Minnowac Wiggler Variant, Gooey Caddis Larva, and a host of other patterns. Later Steve Schweitzer, author of *A Fly Fishing Guide to Rocky Mountain National Park*, became his mentor. Hise began teaching himself how to tie flies. Today he runs his own shop, Casters, located in Hickory, NC.

Hise has been a noted Orvis signature fly designer since 1998. He prefers to tie impressionistic patterns that don't really represent one thing, but rather a wide spectrum of food for fish. Many of his patterns use his favorite material, Australian opossum, in a dubbing loop, which he believes is one of the most versatile dubbing methods.

David Perry
Murfreesboro, TN

David Perry is one of a number of enterprising fly fishermen with the balls to try to make a living guiding and tying flies. So far so good, says the Murfreesboro-based outdoorsman. While his forte is tailwater fishing, Perry also guides and personally fishes a lot in the Great Smoky Mountains. He has developed a number of fly patterns for tailwater and freestone mountain trout stream fishing, with the Bust-A-Brown wet-fly pattern being his favorite. Perry is also a talented writer whose material can be read at www.southeasternfly.com and in *Southern Trout Magazine*.

CHAPTER SEVEN

Waterborne Flies of the Great Smoky Mountains

Over 120 different mayflies live in the waters of the Great Smoky Mountains. This is a male *Stenacron interpunctatum* subimago.
JAY NICHOLS

T he streams of the Great Smoky Mountains National Park (and surrounding waters) have 120 species of Ephemeroptera (mayflies), 111 species of Plecoptera (stoneflies), 7 species of Megaloptera (dobsonflies, fishflies, and alderflies), and 231 species of Trichoptera (caddisflies). This total includes ten species new to science discovered since 2007.

Mayflies

Many species of Ephemeroptera, or "mayflies" according to fly fishermen, occur in various degrees of abundance in the streams of the Great Smoky Mountains. The eastern Nearctic species of the Baetidae genera *Acentrella*, *Acerpenna*, and *Baetis*; the Ephemerellidae genera *Attenella*, *Dannella*, *Drunella*, and *Ephemerella*; the Hep-

Baetis **spp.**

Hendrickson spinner

Maccaffertium **spp.**

Sulphur (*Ephemerella* spp.)

Stenonema femoratum

Anthopotamus spp.

Isonychia sadleri

Tricorythodes spp.

tageniidae genera *Epeorus* and *Maccaffertium*; and the Isonychiidae genus *Isonychia* are especially well represented in the park. Most of the species found in the Smokies are relatively widespread throughout eastern or southeastern North America.

The dominant family group in these waters is that of the clingers. The clingers are so named because their lifestyle is dependent on their ability to cling to gravel and other debris in trout streams. In terms of sheer numbers, they are the most widely available mayfly species found in the waters of the GSMNP. These streams also hold representatives of mayfly families that include what are commonly referred to as crawlers, swimmers, and burrowers.

Although you'd do well to learn about all the different types of mayflies, a few genera of swimmers (a type of mayfly) are exceedingly important to understand if you fly fish these waters. This is especially true of the Slate Drakes or *Isonychia bicolors* as well as several genera of Blue-Winged Olives and Little Blue-Winged Olives. Mayflies in these genera in their various stages of life are key trout foods in these waters through much of the year. However, in the big picture of what you need to know, their relative importance to both trout and fly fishermen is less in the Smokies than on other Western and Northeastern trout streams

Mayfly offspring begin life as nymphs, which reside beneath the surface, clinging to rocks and debris located along the bottom or burrowed in the sand. Usually capable of limited swimming ability, mayfly nymphs live underwater for six to twelve months, and sometimes longer. During that time, they may shed their nymphal outer shell more than one time to accommodate growth. Upon reaching maturity, mayflies emerge to the surface as winged duns. Once airborne, the duns undergo a second metamorphosis, to become breeding adults. Adults return to the streams in great swarms to perform their famous mating dance. Unable to feed because they have no mouth, adult mayflies mate, and then they fall spent on the surface of the water, where waiting trout seize these protein-rich morsels, thus completing the insect's life cycle.

Blue-Winged Olives (Baetidae)

A *Baetis* species fly fishermen fondly refer to as Blue-Winged Olives (BWOs), this example is listed first for two reasons. Most importantly, BWOs are the earliest hatch of the year, often rising in great numbers from the surfaces of streams when ground and water temperatures have reached 40 degrees F. Secondly, BWOs are common to all streams in the park, where they emerge at various elevations during the spring, summer, and fall, even into late autumn. Both the *brunneicolor* and the *intercalaris* species exist in nearly all of these streams, along with other, less-plentiful *Baetis* species.

The body color of the duns ranges from pale olive early in the season to harder olive most other times. Nymphs are tan to olive, and can be brown to olive and sport dark wing pads and three little tails. Spinners are dark, and are sometimes referred to as "Rusty Spinners." Pattern suggestions for the Blue-Winged Olive include

Pheasant Tail Nymph, BWO, Blue Quill Wet, Blue Dun Wet, and Rusty Spinner in hook sizes 18 to 22. Other names given these flies by anglers include Sherry Spinner, Jenny Spinner, July Dun, and Little Claret Dun.

Family Baetidae (Small Minnowflies) Found in the Great Smoky Mountains
Acentrella ampla
Acentrella turbida
Acerpenna pygmaea
Baetis brunneicolor
Baetis intercalaris
Baetis pluto
Baetis tricaudatus

Blue Quills (Leptophlebiidae)

Sometimes referred to as Mahogany Duns or even the *Paraleps* hatch, the Blue Quill is one of the more prolific early season hatches that occurs in the streams of the Great Smoky Mountains. The national park holds a number of different species of Blue Quill, a small mayfly, all of which look pretty much the same to anglers. But the most important aspect of the Blue Quill is that all its species are a favorite food of trout when these aquatic insects are emerging. They are also quite predictable, an attribute not lost on observant fly fishermen. The first hatches usually occur around mid-February, peaking in March and lasting into mid-April, especially at higher elevations. Pattern suggestions for the Blue Quill mayflies include the Blue Quill Nymph and Pheasant Tail Nymph (emerger); Blue Quill, Dark Blue Quill, Mahogany Dun and Compara-dun (dun); and Dark Brown Female Spinner and Blue Quill Spinner (spinner), in hook sizes 14 to 18. Other names given these flies by anglers include Claret Dun and Sepia Dun.

Family Leptophlebiidae (Pronggills) Found in the Great Smoky Mountains
Paraleptophlebia adoptiva
Paraleptophlebia debilis
Paraleptophlebia guttata
Paraleptophlebia mollis
Paraleptophlebia praepedita
Paraleptophlebia strigula
Paraleptophlebia swannanoa

Quill Gordon (Heptageniidae)

Fly fishermen anticipate the Quill Gordon hatch more than any other that occurs in the waters of the Great Smoky Mountains. On most streams it is the first emergence of decent-size flies that old, half-blind men like me can see with any degree of certainty. These are clinger nymphs that demand a swift current in which to live the majority of their lives, although prior to emergence these nymphs migrate from fast-water abodes to slower, generally shallow pools to go airborne. Occasionally these mayflies emerge in large numbers and fill the air above a park stream, but this is not what you can generally expect. You will however, often see a remarkable occurrence of surface feeding when Quill Gordons are about. Also worth noting is that hatches of these mayflies are often localized, sometimes even on single streams. You may encounter a brisk emergence at the end of a long pool, and then not see another for several hundred yards.

Quill Gordon emergences in the waters of the Great Smoky Mountains occur first at lower-elevation streams such as the Oconaluftee River, Twenty-Mile Creek, the Little River, and the West Prong of the Little Pigeon River as early as the second week of February. Brisk hatches occur through March and the first week of April, with some hatches occurring later that month at higher elevations. Patterns designed to match Quill Gordon mayflies include Dark Hare's Ear Nymph, Ginger Quill Wet, Quill Gordon, Gold-Ribbed Hare's Ear Dry, Compara-dun, Rusty Spinner, and Quill Gordon Spinner in hook sizes 12 to 14.

Family Heptageniidae (Flatheaded Mayflies) Found in the Great Smoky Mountains
> *Cinygmula subaequalis*
> *Epeorus dispar*
> *Epeorus pleuralis*
> *Epeorus rubidus*
> *Epeorus subpallidus*

Hendricksons (Ephemerellidae, *Ephemerella subvaria*)

Most experienced fly fishermen around the Great Smoky Mountains refer to Hendricksons as "Red Quills," and these mayflies exist in fair numbers in a handful of streams but are present in virtually all waters. *Ephemerella* species are generally not found in any large numbers, but if you are lucky enough to catch them emerging in good numbers, you should be in for some good fishing, as trout here find them irresistible. The spinnerfall is the most important stage of the Red Quill hatch. Patterns designed to match Red Quill mayflies include the Hendrickson and Dark Hare's Ear Nymph (nymph); Hendrickson, Red Quill Wet, Red Quill, Dark Hendrickson Dun, Light Hendrickson Dun, and Lady Beaverkill Dun (emerger); Rusty Spinner, Mahogany Spinner, and Quill Gordon Spinner (spinner) in hook sizes 10 to 14. Other names given these flies by anglers include Pale Evening Dun and Golden Spinner.

Eastern Blue-Winged Olives (Ephemerellidae, *Drunella*)

Of the many Blue-Winged Olive mayflies found in the waters of the Great Smoky Mountains, the *Drunella* species is the largest in size. These spiny crawler mayflies are usually referred to as Eastern Blue-Winged Olives by local fly fishermen, and they are common to all park waters although they rarely hatch in large numbers at any one time. The closely related Small Eastern Blue-Winged Olives (*Attenella attenuata*) are fairly common in the waters. They hatch on the bottom, however, and should be imitated with BWO patterns in hook size 18. Emergences occur twice a year; some in late summer and early fall, and others during the early winter months. Patterns designed to match Eastern BWO mayflies include the Pheasant Tail, Soft Hackle Black Gnat, and BWO Nymph (nymph); BWO, Parachute BWO, and Compara-dun BWO (emerger); and BWO Parachute and Mahogany Spinner (spinner) in hook sizes 12 to 16.

Family Ephemerellidae (Spiny Crawlers) Found in the Great Smoky Mountains
  Drunella cornuta
  Drunella cornutella
  Drunella lata
  Drunella longicornis
  Drunella tuberculata

Little Blue-Winged Olives (Ephemerellidae)

Park waters also hold some Little Blue-Winged Olives, or *Acentrella* species. These are usually a hook size 20 to 26.

Family Ephemerellidae (Spiny Crawlers) Found in the Great Smoky Mountains
  Ephemerella catawba
  Ephemerella crenula
  Ephemerella hispida
  Ephemerella rossi
  Ephemerella rotunda
  Ephemerella subvaria

Little Sulphur (*Ephemerella dorothea*)

Often referred to as the Eastern Pale Evening Dun, *Ephemerella dorothea* is occasionally encountered in decent numbers on the streams of the Great Smoky Mountains, but it is not a common occurrence. They aren't quite as prolific as the hatches I have fished on Pennsylvania's Spring Creek. These crawler nymphs typically are found in slower waters than generally exist in the park. Patterns designed to match the Little Sulphur mayfly include the Hare's Ear and Little Sulphur Nymph (nymph); Pale Evening Dun and Pale Watery Dun (emerger); and Little Sulphur Spinner and Pale Sulphur Spinner (spinner) in hook sizes 14 to 16.

Leadwing Coachman (Isonychiidae)

Known also as *Isonychia bicolor* or Slate Drakes, these brush-legged mayflies are fairly plentiful in all the streams of the Great Smoky Mountains. These large swimming nymphs (half inch) tend to emerge sporadically along the edges of streams around rocks, and are not usually encountered by fishermen in appreciable concentration throughout the day. Their hatch occurs from early spring through early summer, then again in late summer through early autumn. Spinners fall near dusk or later. Patterns designed to match the Leadwing Coachman mayfly include the Leadwing Coachman Wet (nymph); Leadwing Coachman, Adams, and Dun Variant (emerger); and Rusty Spinner (spinner) in hook sizes 10 to 12.

Family Isonychiidae (Brush-legged Mayflies) Found in the Great Smoky Mountains
  Isonychia serrata
  Isonychia similis

Little Yellow Quills (Heptageniidae)

Often confused with Cahills and sometimes called Pale Evening Duns, these flatheaded mayflies are found in moderate numbers in local streams. Little Yellow Quills are clingers and are most prolific between 3,000 and 4,500-foot elevation where they hatch in the greatest numbers between late summer and early autumn. Patterns designed to match Little Yellow Quills include the Yellow Quill Nymph and Pheasant Tail Nymph (nymph); Little Yellow Quill and Golden Dun (emerger); and Little Yellow Quill Spinner (spinner) in hook sizes 10 to 12.

Family Heptageniidae (Flatheaded Mayflies) Found in the Great Smoky Mountains
  Leucrocuta aphrodite
  Leucrocuta hebe
  Leucrocuta juno
  Leucrocuta minerva
  Leucrocuta thetis

Eastern Green Drakes (Ephemeridae)

Long loved by eastern fly fishermen, the Eastern Green Drake, or *Ephemera guttulata*, is not widely found in the streams of the Great Smoky Mountains. It is included here because it is somewhat unique to Abrams Creek. Emergences of these big burrowing mayflies occur sporadically throughout the day, between late April and late May. Patterns designed to match Eastern Green Drake mayflies include the Green Drake Nymph and Dark Wiggle Nymph (nymph); Dark Green Drake, Eastern Green Drake, and Gray Fox Variant (emerger); and Green Drake Spinner and Mahogany Spinner (spinner) in hook sizes 6 to 10. Other names given these flies by anglers include Gray Drake and Spent Gnat.

Family Ephemeridae (Common Burrowing Mayflies) Found in the Great Smoky Mountains
Ephemera guttulata
Litobrancha recurvata

Brown Drakes (*Ephemera simulans*)

Occasionally you will encounter the Brown Drake mayfly (*Ephemera simulans*). Another burrowing mayfly, these emerge at the same time as the better-known Green Drakes. Patterns designed to match Brown Drake mayflies include the Wiggle Nymph, Marabou Nymph, and Feather Duster (nymph); Brown Drake (emerger); and Brown Drake Spinner, Rusty Spinner, and Mahogany Spinner (spinner) in hook sizes 8 to 10.

American March Browns (Heptageniidae)

The American March Brown, or *Maccaffertium* (formerly *Stenonema*), is an important mayfly hatch in the streams of the Great Smoky Mountains. This species ranks as the most abundant mayfly here according to some old timers. These large clinger nymphs hatch throughout the day beginning in mid-April at lower elevations, and continue almost through June at higher elevations. The spinnerfall, which begins just before dark, is worth waiting for, as this typically triggers brisk feeding on the part of the trout. Patterns designed to match American March Brown mayflies include the Pheasant Tail Nymph, March Brown Nymph, and Hare's Ear Nymph (nymph); American March Brown, Parachute March Brown, and March Brown Compara-dun (emerger); and Red Spinner and Rusty Spinner (spinner) in hook sizes 8 to 10.

Family Heptageniidae (Flatheaded Mayflies) Found in the Great Smoky Mountains
Maccaffertium meririvulanum
Maccaffertium modestum
Maccaffertium pudicum
Maccaffertium sinclairi
Maccaffertium terminatum
Maccaffertium vicarium

Light Cahills (Heptageniidae)

Another important Heptageniidae mayfly family is the *Stenacron interpunctatum*, better known as the Light Cahill. These clinger nymphs reside among rocks where trout can't get to them until they hatch early in the morning and late in the evening. They begin emerging in mid- to late April at lower elevations, and continue to do so at higher elevations through June. Patterns designed to match Little Light Cahills include the Pheasant Tail Nymph and American March Brown Nymph (nymph); Cahill, Light Cahill, and Compara-dun (emerger); and Ginger Quill Spinner (spinner) in hook sizes 10 to 14.

Family Heptageniidae (Flatheaded Mayflies) Found in the Great Smoky Mountains
Stenacron carolina
Stenacron interpunctatum
Stenacron pallidum
Maccaffertium mediopunctatum
Maccaffertium mexicanum integrum
Maccaffertium pulchellum

Cream Cahills (Heptageniidae)

Yet another relatively important *Maccaffertium* is the *Maccaffertium ithaca*, or the so-called Cream Cahills. Most fly fishermen lump them with Light Cahills, as to the untrained eye they look very similar. However, they are slightly lighter in color and hatch in late summer. Patterns designed to match Cream Cahill mayflies include the Pheasant Tail Nymph and American March Brown Nymph (nymph); Cahill, Light Cahill, and Compara-dun (emerger); and Ginger Quill Spinner (spinner) in hook size 14.

Stoneflies

The fast-flowing, well-oxygenated coldwater streams of the Great Smoky Mountains host a cornucopia of stoneflies, or Plecoptera. This Latin name refers to the pleated hind wings that fold under the front wings when the insect is at rest, and is derived from the Greek *pleco,* meaning "folded," and *ptera,* meaning "wing." Plecoptera are a small order of insects of about 2,000 species worldwide.

Stoneflies can be easily recognized by a few simple characteristics. They have three segmented tarsi but their hind legs are not modified for jumping to the extent that Orthoptera's (crickets and grasshoppers) are. Their filiform antennae are at least half the length of the body. The cerci are generally long as well, especially in the aquatic nymphs. The wings are almost always present but are sometimes very short and are folded horizontally back over the body.

The immatures are variously called "nymphs" or "naiads," but are referred to by fly fishermen almost exclusively as nymphs. Stonefly nymphs have three-segmented tarsi. The nymphs always have long cerci and never a third central tail or median caudal filament. Gills, if they have them, can occur on various parts of the thorax and abdomen and are composed only of filaments, not plates. Tracheal gills present as "tufts" behind the head, at the base of legs, or around the anus.

Stoneflies hatch out of the water, crawling to the shoreline or exposed midstream rocks in quiet-water areas. At this time when stonefly nymphs move from fast-water areas to slower emergence zones, they can get caught in the stream's current and become available to hungry trout. Unlike mayflies, which die soon after they emerge, stoneflies live for a relatively long time out of the water. Adults are able to eat and drink

Plecoptera nymph

Early Black Stonefly

Golden Stonefly

Yellow Sally

as adults. In the Great Smoky Mountains adult stoneflies seem to really like ganging up in streamside bushes and trees. About the only time adult stoneflies are available for the trout is when the females are depositing their eggs, which usually occurs at night.

All nine families of stonefly in the United States are present in varying degrees in the Smokies. This represents well over a hundred different species of stonefly, and doubtless there are others yet to be captured and identified. Most of them are about the same size and shape, although it is important to note there are significant differences in the colors of the nymphs and the adults.

Little Brown Stonefly (Capniidae)

While in the Great Smoky Mountains there are over a half-dozen members of the Allocapania clan, fly fishermen generally lump them into a group nicknamed "Black Snowflies." This family of stoneflies may be observed during the winter months.

They are one of the few species of aquatic insects that emerge when the streams are still extremely cold. Also widely known as Little Brown Stoneflies, the nymphs and adults appear black. As is often true in the waters of the national park, when these insects are active you have better luck fishing nymphs than attempting to imitate adult flies.

These rather small nymphs are 5/16 to 9/16 inches long. Emergence occurs around the second week of February at lower elevations, and continues through the third week of April at higher elevations. Pattern suggestions include the Pheasant Tail Nymph and Catskill Curler (nymph), and Early Brown Stonefly and Brown Elk Wing Caddis (adult) in hook sizes 12 or 18.

Family Capniidae (Winter Stoneflies) Found in the Great Smoky Mountains
Allocapnia aurora
Allocapnia frisoni
Allocapnia fumosa
Allocapnia granulata
Allocapnia recta
Allocapnia rickeri
Allocapnia stannardi
Paracapnia angulata

Black Needle Flies (Leuctridae)

Often confused with adult caddisflies, Black Needle Flies are closely related to Capniidae (both are members of the Taeniopterygidae family). Leuctridae is well represented in the park streams both in numbers and in variety, boasting an astounding fifteen species. Easy to ID, they are only stoneflies with slim, long, needle-shaped bodies and wings that roll around their bodies rather than lie flat on top of their backs.

They are most plentiful in the late summer and fall, right up to the onset of winter in December. Pattern suggestions include the Needle Fly Wet and Needle Stonefly Nymph (nymph), and Early Brown Stonefly and Brown Elk Wing Caddis (adult) in hook sizes 12 or 16.

Family Leuctridae (Black Needle Flies) Found in the Great Smoky Mountains
Leuctra alexanderi
Leuctra biloba
Leuctra carolinensis
Leuctra ferruginea
Leuctra grandis
Leuctra mitchellensis
Leuctra monticola

Leuctra nephophila
Leuctra sibleyi
Leuctra tenuis
Leuctra triloba
Leuctra truncata
Leuctra variabilis
Megaleuctra williamsae
Paraleuctra sara

Little Brown Stonefly (Nemouridae)

Four species of genus *Amphinemura*, yet another branch of the Taeniopterygidae family, can be found in park streams. Also known as Black Forestflies or Little Brown Winter Stoneflies, in park waters they can be brown and black and all shades in between. Blindness awaits those determined to tell the *A. appalachia* from the *A. wui*. They all hatch during the winter or early spring months. Hatches can be quite prolific. Pattern suggestions include the Pheasant Tail Nymph and Catskill Curler (nymph), and Early Brown Stonefly and Brown Elk Wing Caddis (adult) in hook sizes 12 or 18.

Family Nemouridae (Nemourid Stoneflies) Found in the Great Smoky Mountains
Amphinemura appalachia
Amphinemura delosa
Amphinemura nigritta
Amphinemura wui
Prostoia completa
Prostoia similis
Soyedina carolinensis
Soyedina kondratieffi
Zapada chila

Little Green Stonefly (Chloroperlidae)

An adult you just can't miss when it is out and about, the Little Green Stonefly is a brightly colored insect that accounts for at least a half dozen different but closely related species. These bugs emerge in the summer after many other species have already hatched. At lower elevations this occurs in early June, while it can be found happening at elevations above 3,500 feet well into August.

The adults of several of the species are often "apple" green, and at times you will see them in greenish-yellow hues. Pattern suggestions include the Turkey Tail Nymph and Pheasant Tail Nymph (nymph), and Little Green Stonefly and Yellow Sally (adult) in hook sizes 14 or 18.

Family Chloroperlidae (Green Stoneflies) Found in the Great Smoky Mountains
   Alloperla atlantica
   Alloperla caudata
   Alloperla chloris
   Alloperla nanina
   Alloperla neglecta
   Alloperla usa
   Haploperla brevis
   Rasvena terna
   Suwallia marginata
   Sweltsa lateralis
   Sweltsa mediana
   Sweltsa urticae

Little Yellow Stonefly (Perlodidae)

Affectionately referred to as the Little Yellow Stonefly, these members of the *Isoperla* genus of the Perlodidae family account for at least ten species in the waters of the Great Smoky Mountains. A popular nickname, here and elsewhere, the term "Yellow Sally" applies to several other species as well. They rank high among the most plentiful groups of stoneflies in these streams. Yellow Sallies usually hatch in the afternoon and usually begin to deposit their eggs late in the afternoon prior to dark. Emergences begin around the first week of May at lower elevations, and continue to around mid-July at high elevations. Pattern suggestions include the Catskill Curler Nymph and Pheasant Tail Nymph (nymph), and Yellow Stimulator and Yellow Sally (adult) in hook sizes 10 or 16.

Family Perlodidae (Perlodid Stoneflies) Found in the Great Smoky Mountains
   Clioperla clio
   Cultus decisus isolatus
   Cultus verticalis
   Diploperla duplicata
   Diploperla robusta
   Helopicus subvarians
   Isogenoides hansoni
   Isoperla bellona
   Isoperla dicala
   Isoperla distincta
   Isoperla frisoni
   Isoperla holochlora
   Isoperla lata
   Isoperla orata

Isoperla similis
Malirekus hastatus
Oconoperla innubila
Remenus bilobatus
Yugus arinus
Yugus bulbosus

Little Yellow Summer Stonefly (Peltoperlidae)

Known to some as the Mahogany and to others as the Roach Fly, this fairly large family is well represented in the waters of the Great Smoky Mountains as well as in other freestone mountain streams from northern Virginia to northern Georgia. Little Yellow Summer Stonefly emergences begin around the first week of May at lower elevations, and continue to around mid-July at high elevations. Pattern suggestions include the Catskill Curler Nymph and Pheasant Tail Nymph (nymph), and Yellow Stimulator and Yellow Sally (adult) in hook sizes 12 or 18.

Family Peltoperlidae (Roachlike Stoneflies) Found in the Great Smoky Mountains
Tallaperla anna
Tallaperla cornelia
Tallaperla elisa
Tallaperla laurie
Tallaperla maria
Viehoperla ada

Golden Stonefly (Perlidae)

Held in the highest esteem by many fly fishermen familiar with the waters of the Great Smoky Mountains, the jumbo-sized aquatic insects referred to as Golden Stoneflies are appropriately named. This group is arguably the most plentiful stonefly in park waters. Most of these are very colorful as nymphs, while adults range from a golden dull yellow color to a solid brown depending on the species. Hatches occur at lower elevations in early May, and end at higher elevations around the end of May. Pattern suggestions include the Golden Stonefly Nymph, Eastern Yellow Stonefly, and Bird's Stonefly Nymph (nymph); and Orange Stimulator, Improved Sofa Pillow, and Downwing Hornberg (adult) in hook sizes 4 or 10.

Family Perlidae (Common Stoneflies) Found in the Great Smoky Mountains
Acroneuria abnormis
Acroneuria arida
Acroneuria carolinensis
Acroneuria filicis
Acroneuria frisoni

Acroneuria perplexa
Acroneuria petersi
Agnetina capitata
Attaneuria ruralis
Beloneuria georgiana
Beloneuria stewarti
Eccoptura xanthenes
Hansonoperla appalachia
Neoperla occipitalis
Paragnetina ichusa
Paragnetina immarginata
Perlesta frisoni
Perlesta nelsoni
Perlinella drymo
Perlinella ephyre

Giant Stoneflies (Pteronarcyidae)

Giant black stoneflies are quite plentiful in most of the streams of the Great Smoky Mountains, where they find picture-perfect habitat due to outstanding water quality with high dissolved-oxygen content. Of the three species found here, *Pteronarcys dorsata* is the most common. These brown to black nymphs are huge (up to 2½ inches long) and live for three or four years in their aquatic world. Big trout are often taken on fly patterns that imitate these colossal nymphs during the day at peak hatch periods, even though peaks occur in late evening. You can find spent adults most often at the ends of the runs and heads of the pools. Pattern suggestions include the Kevin's Stonefly Nymph, Kaufmann's Stonefly Nymph, and Black Woolly Bugger (nymph); and Black Stimulator and Bird's Stonefly (adult) in hook sizes 4 or 10.

Family Pteronarcyidae (Giant Stoneflies) Found in the Great Smoky Mountains

Pteronarcys dorsata
Pteronarcys proteus
Pteronarcys scotti

Early Dark Stonefly (Taeniopterygidae)

Referred to by a variety of nicknames that include Early Dark Stonefly, Little Brown Stonefly, or Black Winter Stonefly, these are perhaps the most confusing of all Plecoptera found in the waters of the Great Smoky Mountains. Most of these stoneflies are collectively called Little Browns, as the adults are both brown and black as well as all shades in between. They hatch during the winter or early spring months and often in large quantities. Pattern suggestions include the Early Brown Stonefly Nymph, Pheasant Tail Nymph, and Catskill Curler (nymph); and Early Brown Stonefly and Elk Caddis (adult) in hook sizes 12 or 18.

Family Taeniopterygidae (Early Dark Stonefly) Found in the Great Smoky Mountains

Bolotoperla rossi

Oemopteryx contorta

Strophopteryx fasciata

Strophopteryx limata

Taenionema atlanticum

Taeniopteryx burksi

Taeniopteryx maura

Caddisflies

Literature regarding fly fishing for trout in the Great Smoky Mountains has long been tilted towards mayflies, so it is easy for unknowing anglers to overlook the importance of caddisflies. However, the caddisfly does not take a backseat to the more highly touted mayfly in the local food chain. To date, 230 species of caddisflies have been recorded in the national park. One caddisfly species is apparently restricted solely to the park. The recently described *Neophylax kolodskii* is known from just a few streams deep in the interior

Early Black Caddis

October Caddis

Grannom

In many ways mayflies and caddisflies are very similar. Each breeds as a winged adult and lays its eggs in water. Upon hatching, the differences in these two aquatic insects are at their most evident. Caddisflies, like mayflies, begin life as waterborne subadults. Caddisfly offspring, however, are what biologists refer to as pupae, not nymphs. Whereas a mayfly nymph is a well-armored creature complete with legs and most other visible attributes of an insect, a caddisfly pupa usually looks like a plump, soft little inch-long worm resembling a common grub. The caddisfly pupa is still endowed with all of the tools needed not only to survive in the hostile sur-roundings of a trout stream, but also to prosper. Caddisfly pupae construct "houses" for themselves that protect them from most predators.

Some caddisfly houses are constructed of sticks and leaves, while others rely on tiny pebbles and even sand. These sticks, leaves, pebbles, and sand are held together by secretions produced by the caddisfly pupa. One large group of caddisflies in the park constructs netlike seines, which they use to capture their food. You can find the caddisfly pupae still occupying their abodes if you turn over boulders and pick up the submerged sticks used by these creatures to secure their homes.

Mayflies and caddisflies emerge in a similar manner. Maximum reproduction is facilitated by peak emergences of ready-to-breed adult flies. Sedges, as adult caddis-flies are called, rarely ride the surface as long as mayfly duns. Emerging sedges skit-ter upstream along the surface in a rapid, erratic fashion. This makes them far more difficult for trout to nab than a stodgy dun that rides along the moving surface wait-ing for its waxy wings to sufficiently dry for it to become airborne. Many times, peak emergences of caddisflies are difficult to see, while peak emergences of mayflies are more visible.

Trout in the Smokies tend to prey on caddisfly pupae just under the surface, where these small aquatic insects struggle to shuck their pupal husk. The pupae are highly vulnerable for several minutes during their efforts to emerge, providing trout with easy pickings. However, except for an occasional dorsal or tail fin breaking the surface, it is difficult to spot the darting movement of a trout helping itself to a mass emerging of caddisfly pupae.

Unlike mayflies and stoneflies, caddisflies undergo complete metamorphoses. They start as eggs and hatch to become larvae. They then morph into pupae before the final transition into adults ready to emerge. Caddisfly larvae are classified according to their lifestyle and dwelling. They can be either cased or uncased. The larvae can be further split into five groups: free-living caddises, net spinners, saddle case builders, purse case builders, and tube case builders. Actually there are nine groups, but these five are of greatest interest to fly fishermen. With or without shielding, they resemble maggots.

Larvae mature to the pupal stage, but only for a short time. Cased caddis are out-side of their protective homes at this time, and must find a protective nook where they remain until emergence. Ready-to-emerge pupae, or pharate adults, are fully formed, save for a thin membrane that compresses their wings to them. This stage after caddis pupae leave their cases but before they become airborne interests fly fishermen greatly, as this is when caddis are most vulnerable to hungry trout.

The lucky ones make it to the surface, where their wings sprout for the terrestrial portion of their lives. Most wiggle their way to the surface to go airborne, but several species head to the edge of the water to climb free from the killing zone. Mating quickly ensues in streamside greenery, on rocks, and on other structures near the water. Once fertilized, the females return to their native waters to deposit their eggs. Some species simply drop off their eggs, while others skip the surface before diving back into the water to deposit their eggs. As with mayflies, successful mating is the final act for these bugs.

Ironically, surface-riding caddisfly patterns such as the Picket Fence, Elk Wing Caddis, Orange Palmer, Royal Trude, Chuck Caddis, or Greenbrier Special series often produce more strikes when surface caddisfly activity is not especially brisk. Admittedly, these dry-fly patterns produce best at streams and rivers where caddis-flies occupy a prominent position in the food chain. However, in my opinion, many times current-riding caddisfly patterns serve just as well as prospecting flies, such as a Royal Coachman, as they do traditional hatch-matching imitators.

Caddisfly emergence imitators can usually be fished up- or downstream, depending mostly on stream clarity and size. When fly fishing smallish to medium-sized, gin-clear mountain rivulets, cast upstream and allow the current to deliver your offering. This technique requires mending your line to ensure a natural drift as well as the ability to efficiently set the hook when a strike occurs. Casting upstream is essential in small, clear streams where your presence upstream from trout facing into the current would foil your efforts.

American Grannon (Brachycentridae)

Often locally referred to collectively as Little Black Caddis, and as the "Mother's Day Hatch" by some, Brachycentridae, genus *Brachycentrus*, has three key species in the waters of the Great Smoky Mountains. An important hatch fly fishermen should learn to recognize, Little Black Caddis are found in all park streams and emerge around the third week in February at lower elevations and mid- to late April at higher elevations. These caddisflies hatch during the afternoon when the water is 48–52 degrees F.

Their chimney-style houses attached to submerged rocks are easily recognizable. Emerging pupae swim to the surface to hatch, and adults skitter on the surface to become airborne. They deposit their eggs starting mid-afternoon until dark. Pattern suggestions include the Brassie (larvae); Deep Sparkle Pupa (pupa); Emerging Sparkle Pupa and Compara-dun Emerger (emerger); Deer Hair Caddis and Elk Wing Caddis (newly hatched adult); and Deer Hair Caddis, Grouse and Green, and Leadwing Coach Wet (returning adult) in hook sizes 16 or 18.

Family Brachycentridae (Short-horned Caddisflies) Found in the Great Smoky Mountains

Brachycentrus spinae
Micrasema bennetti
Micrasema burksi
Micrasema charonis
Micrasema rickeri
Micrasema rusticum
Micrasema scotti
Micrasema wataga

Green Rock Worm Caddis (Rhyacophilidae)

Often called the Green Sedge, genus *Rhyacophila* accounts for twenty-one known species in the Great Smoky Mountains, making these waters some of the most diverse for these caddisflies in the entire world. Many fly fishermen collectively refer to them as Green Rock Worms because they appear as such during the larval stage, at which point the insects can occasionally be found in a variety of streams in the Great Smoky Mountains. Their abundance appears scattered, with a few found in Big Creek, while Abrams Creek has a substantial quantity of Green Rock Worm Caddis.

Unlike most of the Trichoptera found in the Great Smoky Mountains, Green Sedges are not long-term house builders, but rather free-living larvae that reside in fast runs and riffles where they are readily taken by trout year-round. The larval stage is by far the most important stage to imitate. Emergences begin in late April at lower elevations, and last well into July at higher elevations. They seem to peak Memorial Day Weekend at Abrams Creek, where they are a dominant hatch. Pattern suggestions include the Green Rock Worm (larva); Sparkle Pupa and Green (pupa); Emergent Sparkle Pupa and Compara-dun Emerger (emerger); Deer Hair Caddis and Elk Wing Caddis (newly hatched adult); and Deer Hair Caddis, Grouse and Green, and Leadwing Coach Wet (returning adult) in hook sizes 8 or 16.

Family Rhyacophilidae (Free-living Caddisflies) Found in the Great Smoky Mountains

Rhyacophila accola
Rhyacophila acutiloba
Rhyacophila amicis
Rhyacophila appalachia
Rhyacophila atrata
Rhyacophila carolina
Rhyacophila carpenteri
Rhyacophila fuscula
Rhyacophila glaberrima

Rhyacophila minor
Rhyacophila montana
Rhyacophila mycta
Rhyacophila nigrita
Rhyacophila teddyi
Rhyacophila torva

Little Short-Horned Sedge (Glossosomatidae)

Several species of Little Short-Horned Sedge are well represented in the Smokies, with *Glossosoma nigrior* being the most widespread and abundant. The sedges are fairly plentiful in some of the streams. These are saddle-cased larvae, which means they are most important to fly fishermen as emergers. They begin hatching in late March at lower elevations, and continue to be plentiful well into mid-June at higher elevations.

Pattern suggestions include the Buck Skin Caddis Nymph, Cream Larva, and Pink Larva (larvae); Deep Sparkle Pupa (pupa); Emergent Sparkle Pupa and Compara-dun Emerger (emerger); Deer Hair Caddis and Elk Wing Caddis (newly hatched adult); and Dancing Caddis (returning adult) in hook sizes 18 or 22.

Family Glossosomatidae (Tortoiseshell Case Makers) Found in the Great Smoky Mountains

Agapetus crasmus
Agapetus illini
Agapetus pinatus
Agapetus rossi
Agapetus tomus
Glossosoma nigrior

Cinnamon Caddis (Hydropsychidae)

Often referred to as Spotted Sedges, genus *Ceratopsyche* comprises a large group of species of caddisflies known as "net spinners," seven of which are represented in the Great Smoky Mountains National Park. It is believed that the genus *Hydropsyche* contributes an additional nine closely related species of caddisfly. Most common at Abrams Creek, Spotted Sedges are rarely encountered elsewhere in great numbers.

Pattern suggestions include the Caddis Larva olive/brown (larva), Deep Sparkle Pupa olive/tan (pupa), Emergent Sparkle Pupa and Compara-dun Emerger (emerger), Cinnamon Fluttering Caddis and W. B. Caddis (newly hatched adult), and Cinnamon Caddis and March Brown Wet (returning adult) in hook sizes 12 to 18.

Family Hydropsychidae (Common Net Spinners) Found in the Great Smoky Mountains
Arctopsyche irrorata
Ceratopsyche alhedra
Ceratopsyche bronta
Ceratopsyche macleodi
Ceratopsyche morosa
Ceratopsyche slossonae
Ceratopsyche sparna
Diplectrona metaqui
Diplectrona modesta
Homoplectra doringa
Hydropsyche betteni
Hydropsyche carolina
Hydropsyche depravata
Hydropsyche rossi
Hydropsyche venularis
Parapsyche apicalis
Parapsyche cardis

Little Olive Caddis (*Cheumatopsyche*)

Locally referred to by most fly fishermen as the Little Sister Sedge, the net-spinning Little Olive Caddis, *Cheumatopsyche*, are represented in the Great Smoky Mountains by no fewer than a dozen species. They are quite small and are found in most streams, but only at Abrams Creek are they found in an appreciable concentration. They emerge between late April and mid-July. It is best to imitate the pupal stage of this caddisfly.

Pattern suggestions include the Caddis Larva olive/brown and Olive Larva (larva), Deep Sparkle Pupa olive/tan (pupa), Emergent Sparkle Pupa and Compara-dun Emerger (emerger), Olive Fluttering Caddis (newly hatched adult), and Elk Wing Caddis and Greenbrier Special (returning adult) in hook sizes 18 to 22.

Genus *Cheumatopsyche* (Little Olive Caddis) Found in the Great Smoky Mountains
Cheumatopsyche campyla
Cheumatopsyche harwoodi
Cheumatopsyche helma
Cheumatopsyche pasella
Cheumatopsyche speciosa

Great Brown Autumn Sedge (Limnephilidae)

The Limnephilidae family of caddisflies, genus *Pycnopsyche*, is represented by ten members in the streams of the park. From a fly-fishing prospective, the Great Brown

Autumn Sedge, or Northern Caddisfly as it is also called, is certainly worth knowing. Hatches of these large caddisflies occur first in mid-September and last almost until Christmas when the weather is mild. One of the more important, larger caddisflies, the Great Brown Autumn Sedge has a cinnamon-colored body and brown to yellowish-brown wings.

Pattern suggestions include the Strawman and Cased Caddis Larva (larva); Slow-Water Pupa and Amber Deep Sparkle Pupa (pupa); Emergent Sparkle Pupa and Compara-dun Emerger (emerger); Elk Wing Caddis, Pheasant Caddis, and Giant Orange Caddis (newly hatched adult); and Amber Slow-Water Caddis and Orange Snipe Dry (returning adult) in hook sizes 8 to 12.

Family Limnephilidae (Northern Caddisflies) Found in the Great Smoky Mountains

Frenesia difficilis

Hydatophylax argus

Ironoquia punctatissima

Platycentropus radiatus

Pseudostenophylax uniformis

Pycnopsyche antica

Pycnopsyche conspersa

Pycnopsyche divergens

Pycnopsyche flavata

Pycnopsyche gentilis

Pycnopsyche guttifer

Pycnopsyche lepida

Pycnopsyche limbata

Pycnopsyche luculenta

Pycnopsyche scabripennis

Pycnopsyche sonso

Pycnopsyche subfasciata

Long Horn Sedges (Leptoceridae)

Long Horn Sedges (sometimes called Dark Long Horned Caddis) are most common in Abrams Creek, which has well over a dozen different species of this caddisfly. However, for the most part these caddisflies are bit players in the world of fly fishing in the Smokies. These borrowers hatch between mid-April and mid-June in sporadic, undramatic fashion in the slowest water where you are likely to cast.

Pattern suggestions include the Stickbait Pupa (larva); Deep Sparkle Pupa brown (pupa); Emergent Sparkle Pupa and Compara-dun Emerger (emerger); Elk Wing Caddis, Deer Hair Caddis, and Henryville Special Caddis (newly hatched adult); and Dark Deer Hair Caddis (returning adult) in hook sizes 14 to 18.

Family Leptoceridae (Long Horned Caddisflies) Found in the Great Smoky Mountains
Ceraclea ancylus
Ceraclea cancellata
Ceraclea tarsipunctata
Mystacides sepulchralis
Oecetis inconspicua
Oecetis nocturna
Oecetis persimilis
Setodes stehri
Triaenodes abus
Triaenodes ignitus
Triaenodes taenius
Triaenodes tardus

Little Gray Sedge (Goeridae)

Also commonly known as Summer Fliers, Little Gray Sedges are *Goera* species of the large Limnephilidae family, which represent at least four species in these waters. Little Gray Sedges have dull yellow bodies and tannish-gray wings. Many local anglers just refer to them as "tan caddis." They hatch in the late spring in the riffles. These caddisflies can hatch in large quantities at various streams in the park. Pattern suggestions include the Brassie, Strawman, and Cased Caddis Larva (larva); Deep Sparkle Pupa brown/ginger (pupa); Emergent Sparkle Pupa and Compara-dun Emerger (emerger); Elk Wing Caddis and King's River Caddis (newly hatched adult); and W. D. Caddis and Deer Hair Caddis (returning adult) in hook sizes 6 to 18.

Family Goeridae (Goerid Caddisflies) Found in the Great Smoky Mountains
Goera calcarata
Goera fuscula
Goerita flinti
Goerita semata

White Miller Caddisfly (Leptoceridae, Nectopsyche)

A lot of the really old-time fly fishermen referred to any light-colored caddisfly adult as a White Miller. Two species of these long-horned caddisflies are found in Great Smoky Mountains streams, and they are easy to distinguish from other caddisflies. The antennae are about one-and-a-half times their body length. They are also found in moderately flowing streams, especially those with heavy weeds or other aquatic vegetation. Hesse Creek has the most White Millers I have observed.

These caddisflies hatch two times a year; once in the spring and again in late summer to early autumn, although it is generally an occurrence of limited interest to fly fishermen here due to their relative scarcity in many park streams. Pattern suggestions include the Strawman (larva), White Miller Soft Hackle (pupa), Emergent Sparkle Pupa and Compara-dun Emerger (emerger), White Miller X-Caddis and Fluttering White Miller (newly hatched adult), and Deer Hair Caddis (returning adult) in hook sizes 12 to 18.

Other Families of Caddisfly

Several other families of caddisfly are of less interest to fly fishermen in the Great Smoky Mountains, but you may see some of them on rare occasions.

Family Apataniidae (*Apatania* Caddisflies)
Apatania praevolans

Family Dipseudopsidae (Pitottube Net Spinners)
Phylocentropus carolinus
Phylocentropus lucidus

Family Hydroptilidae (Microcaddisflies)
Hydroptila callia
Hydroptila delineata
Hydroptila hamata
Hydroptila remita
Hydroptila talladega
Neotrichia minutisimella
Palaeagapetus celsus
Stactobiella delira
Stactobiella martynovi

Family Lepidostomatidae (Scalemouth Caddisflies)
Lepidostoma americanum
Lepidostoma bryanti
Lepidostoma carrolli
Lepidostoma compressum
Lepidostoma excavatum
Lepidostoma flinti
Lepidostoma frosti
Lepidostoma griseum
Lepidostoma latipenne
Lepidostoma lobatum
Lepidostoma lydia
Lepidostoma modestum

Lepidostoma ontario
Lepidostoma pictile
Lepidostoma serratum
Lepidostoma styliferum
Lepidostoma tibiale
Lepidostoma togatum
Theliopsyche corona
Theliopsyche epilonis
Theliopsyche grisea

Family Molannidae (Hoodcase Maker)
Molanna blenda

Family Odontoceridae (Toothed Horn Caddisflies)
Pseudogoera singularis
Psilotreta amera
Psilotreta frontalis
Psilotreta labida
Psilotreta rossi
Psilotreta rufa

Family Philopotamidae (Fingernet Caddisflies)
Chimarra obscura
Dolophilodes distinctus
Dolophilodes major
Wormaldia moesta
Wormaldia mohri

Family Phryganeidae (Giant Case Makers)
Agrypnia vestita
Oligostomis pardalis
Ptilostomis ocellifera

Family Polycentropodidae (Trumpet and Tubenet Caddisflies)
Cyrnellus fraternus
Nyctiophylax banksi
Nyctiophylax moestus
Nyctiophylax nephophilus
Polycentropus carlsoni
Polycentropus carolinensis
Polycentropus cinereus

Polycentropus colei
Polycentropus confusus
Polycentropus maculatus
Polycentropus rickeri

Family Psychomyiidae (Nettube Caddisflies)
Lype diversa
Psychomyia flavida
Psychomyia nomada

Family Sericostomatidae (Bushtailed Case Makers)
Agarodes tetron
Fattigia pele

Family Uenoidae (*Neophylax* Caddisflies)
Neophylax concinnus
Neophylax consimilis
Neophylax mitchelli
Neophylax oligius
Neophylax ornatus

Family Calamoceratidae (Hollowstick Case Makers)
Anisocentropus pyraloides
Heteroplectron americanum

Family Helicopsychidae (Snail Shell Case Makers)
Helicopsyche borealis

The Family Megaloptera

This is a small family, with fewer than three hundred species known worldwide, and fewer than fifty species known from North America. Seven species of Megaloptera have been collected in the Great Smoky Mountains. One, Alderfly (*Sialis joppa Ross*), was collected in the Newfound Gap area of the national park, the only place it has ever been collected in park waters. The species are widespread in eastern North America. A total of eighteen species of Megaloptera inhabit the Carolinas, so some aquatic entomologists speculate that two or three additional species of this order may be found in the park's waters.

In terms of relative abundance and importance to the trout and smallmouth bass of the Great Smoky Mountains, Megaloptera are bit players. However, gamefish relish the larval and nymph forms of these aquatic insects, and as such, even though they aren't as plentiful as other insects, they are still important to know and understand. Foremost among them are the crane flies. You can find them in the streams of the Great Smoky Mountains and trout definitely feed on them in the larval and adult stages of life.

Summer Fishflies

Summer Fishflies (*Chauliodes pectinicornis*), also known as dobsonflies, are worth noting because they are desirable to trout. Their large larvae are aquatic omnivores: they can be detritivores (detritus eaters) or herbivores, and also prey on other invertebrates. Larvae tend to live in calm bodies of water with lots of debris, but they leave the water to pupate under bark and inside rotting logs. Pupation takes approximately ten days. Adults emerge to mate and live perhaps a week. There appears to be just one flight per year, and their life cycle may be just one year, though old timers swear they have a two- to three-year life cycle. They lay their eggs in masses on vegetation near still bodies of water, from which larvae hatch and crawl to the water.

During the larval stage, fishflies look like fat worms. The adults have a skinny body and very long legs. We called the larvae "grampuses" growing up, while most others refer to the feisty worms as hellgrammites. They spend most of their life in the larval stage. Other nicknames for the hellgrammites include "go-devils" and "crawlerbottoms." The larvae reach to 2 to 3 inches in length, with gills all along the sides of their segmented bodies that allow them to extract oxygen from water. Built to prey on other insect larvae, fishflies sport short, sharp mandibles on their heads, with which they can also inflict painful bites on fingers. When it's time, the larvae crawl out onto land and pupate. They stay in their cocoons over the winter and emerge only to mate.

Dragonflies

One of the most fascinating aquatic insects, dragonflies are occasionally found in the Great Smoky Mountains National Park. Their nicknames include the "devil's darning needle" and the old Welsh name "gwas-y-neidr," meaning the "adder's servant." Dragonflies can sometimes be mistaken for damselflies, which are morphologically similar; however, you can tell adults apart by the fact that the wings of most dragonflies are held away from, and perpendicular to, the body when at rest. Dragonflies are some of the fastest insects in the world in flight, but although they possess six legs (like any other insect), most of them cannot walk well.

Dragonflies deposit their eggs in the water. Once the eggs hatch, the life cycle of a dragonfly larva begins as a nymph. A nymph looks like a little alien creature: it hasn't grown its wings yet and has what looks like a crusty hump hanging onto its back. Dragonfly nymphs live in the water while they grow and develop, which can take up to four years to complete. If the nymph cycle is completed in the beginning of the wintertime, they will remain in the water until spring when it is warm enough.

Dragonfly nymphs live in the calmest areas of streams, meaning they are more abundant at lower elevations than in headwater rills. They are not plentiful in many areas of the national park.

One of the great mysteries of the Great Smoky Mountains National Park involves the saga of the Williamson's emerald dragonfly (*Somatochlora williamsoni*). Its current status is that of "missing," having been last seen here in the 1940s. According to the story, scientists working in the park then captured this beautiful dragonfly as it buzzed through orchards just above Twin Creeks (now a Science Center on Cherokee Orchard Road). It has not been seen since then, despite repeated searches. One reason may be habitat change from orchards and fields to dense forest. If you see this dragonfly let the rangers know about it.

Damselflies

Although damselflies are in the same order as dragonflies, adults are slender and more delicate in appearance than their more robust and swifter cousins. As a kid we called them "snake feeders" and often tried with little success to catch these agile speedsters. Like the rest of their kin, damselflies have a simple metamorphosis, including an aquatic nymph stage. It takes ten to fifteen molts for the nymphs to emerge and transform into the aerial adult stage, although most damselflies can accomplish this transformation in one year. The nymphs have three caudal lamellae (gills) attached to the end of the abdomen. Most damselfly nymphs are predators; some are scavengers as well. Like dragonflies, damselflies are not plentiful in the waters of the Great Smoky Mountains. They prefer still to slow-moving water and are of questionable importance to fly fishermen.

The Family Chironomidae (Midge flies)

I actually debated skipping the true flies in this book, as they are generally of more interest to southern tailwater river fly fishermen. However, for the sake of completeness, I've decided to include them. Commonly known as midges (order Diptera, family Chironomidae), true flies account for most of the benthos macroinvertebrates in freshwater. In many aquatic habitats this group constitutes more than half of the total number of aquatic insect species present. This is not the case in the Great Smoky Mountains, where midges are of marginal importance to most fly fishermen, at least compared to the importance of midges in the nearby Clinch River tailwaters.

The family is also the most widely distributed group of insects. The larvae, recognizable from their anterior and posterior pairs of prolegs, are diverse in form and size. The Chironomidae, commonly known as nonbiting midges, comprise a large, cosmopolitan family whose adults are small and delicate and superficially resemble mosquitoes. The larvae are generally large (½ inch) and are red colored, hence the term "bloodworm." The red color is due to the presence of hemoglobin that stores oxygen. These larvae exchange oxygen across their cuticle and some forms of larvae have tubular gills extending ventrally near the caudal end. These tube makers create a current in the tubes in which they live by undulating their bodies so that water passes through. Adult midges are minute to medium-sized winged insects that often emerge, simultaneously, in huge numbers. Some species are uni- or bivoltine, but can produce up to four broods in a year, while others take more than one year to complete their life cycles.

Midges are important sources of food for trout in the Great Smoky Mountains, but a lot of fly fishermen avoid the tiny imitations that match the hatch. These almost invisible flies, coupled with trout you rarely see, can amount to frustrating fishing. The midges of the Great Smoky Mountains occur in many sizes and colors. For the purpose of fly fishing in these waters, the most important stage of the midge is the pupa.

For most of their life the larvae stay hidden in burrows they create. When the larvae morph into the pupal stage, they are quite vulnerable and readily eaten by trout. Trout can position themselves in one place and still be able to eat all the pupae they want when the flies hatching. Trout will only rarely eat the full-grown adults from the surface because the pupae are so easily taken.

CHAPTER EIGHT

Hatches and Matches for Aquatic Insects

Time of year and time of day should both influence your selection of flies. LOUIS CAHILL

Late-Winter Hatches and Matches for Aquatic Insects (January/February)

Common & Latin Names	Emergence Days	Time of Day	Hook Size	Matching Dry Patterns	Matching Nymph/ Wet Patterns
Blue-Winged Olive *Baetis vagans*	Late January– February	Midday	14-18	Male Adams Royal Wulff Adams Parachute	My Pet Beadhead Hare's Ear
Blue Quill *Paraleptophebia adoptiva*	Late February	Late morning/ midafternoon	16	Adams Variant Thunderhead Blue Quill Dark Brown Spinner	Yallarhammar Solomon's Black Pupa Beadhead Zug Bug George Nymph
Little Black Caddis *Chimarra aterrima*	January and February	Late morning/ afternoon	14-18	Elk Wing Caddis Bucktail Caddis Adams Caddis	Little Black Caddis Pupa Beadhead Nymph
Little Black Stonefly *Allocapnia aurora*	January– February	All day	16-18	Little Black Stone Black Caddis	Woolly Bugger Black Stonefly Nymph Bitch Creek
Winter Black Stonefly *Capnia vernalis*	January– February	All day (see nymphs)	18-20	Little Black Stone Black Caddis	Black Stonefly Nymph Montana Stonefly
Early Brown Stonefly (or Dark Stonefly) *Strophopteryx fasciata*	Mid- to late February	Midday	14-16	Deer Hair Caddis Pickett Fence Little Brown Stone Dark Elk Wing Caddis	Yallarhammar Brown Stonefly Bitch Creek
Olive Midge *Dixella* spp.	January– February	Midday	18-20	Adams Variant Griffith's Gnat	Hare's Ear

Early Spring Hatches and Matches for Aquatic Insects (March/April)

Common & Latin Names	Emergence Days	Time of Day	Hook Size	Matching Dry Patterns	Matching Nymph/ Wet Patterns
Blue-Winged Olive *Baetis vagans*	March–May	Midday	14-18	Male Adams	Beadhead My Pet
Red Quill *Ephemerella subvaria*	Late March– mid-April	Late afternoon	12-16	Red Quill Hendrickson Male Adams	Hendrickson Nymph Beadhead Muskrat
Quill Gordon *Epeorus pleuralis*	Early March– early April (later at higher elevations)	Midday	12-16	Male Adams Quill Gordon Royal Wulff Tennessee Wulff	Beadhead Hare's Ear Gordon Nymph Flashback Hare's Ear
March Brown *Maccaffertium vicarium (Stenonema vicarium)*	Mid-March– April	Midday	12-16	March Brown Royal Wulff	Hare's Ear March Brown Nymph
Gray Fox *Stenonema fuscum*	Mid-April– late April	Mid- to late afternoon	14	Gray Fox Ginger Quill Gray Fox Variant	Beadhead Hare's Ear My Pet Secret Weapon
Green Drake *Ephemera guttulata*	Last week of April	Late afternoon to evening	8-12	Green Drake Paradrake White Wulff Coffin Fly	Green Drake Nymph Beadhead My Pet My Pet Green Nymph Eastern Green Drake Nymph
Light Cahill *Stenonema ithaca*	Late April	Afternoon to evening	12-16	Light Cahill Hazel Creek Jim Charley	Cotton Top Nymph George Nymph Cahill Nymph
Dark Dun/Black Caddis *Brachycentrus americanus*	Mid-April	Midmorning	14-16	Black Soft Hackle Tan Caddis Henryville Dark Elk Hair Caddis Yellow Palmer (green tied)	Streaker (Stickbait) Yallarhammar Beadhead Hare's Ear Secret Weapon

(continued on page 88)

Early Spring Hatches and Matches for Aquatic Insects (March/April) (continued)

Common & Latin Names	Emergence Days	Time of Day	Hook Size	Matching Dry Patterns	Matching Nymph/ Wet Patterns
Green/Apple Green Caddis *Rhyacophila* spp.	Late April	Mid-to-late morning	14-18	Greenbrier Special Olive Caddis	Beadhead Zug Bug Green Tellico Nymph Secret Weapon Rockworm Caddis
Little Black Caddis *Chimarra aterrima*	March–April	Late morning/ afternoon	14-18	Elk Wing Caddis Bucktail Caddis Adams Caddis	Yallarhammar Beadhead Pupa My Pet
Little Yellow Stonefly (or Tawny Stonefly) *Isoperla bilineata*	Late March– April	Midday	12-16	Bucktail Caddis Yellow Palmer Jim Charley Elk Wing Caddis Greenbrier Special Little Yellow Stone	Yallarhammar George Nymph Beadhead Cotton Top Brooks Golden Stone Little Stonefly Nymph Brassie
Giant Black Stonefly *Pteronarcys scotti*	Late March– April	Early morning	12-14	Giant Black Stone	Dark Stonefly Crown Nymph Montana Nymph Black Stonefly Nymph Bitch Creek
Olive Midge *Dixella* spp.	March–April	Midday	18-20	Adams Variant Griffith's Gnat	Beadhead Hare's Ear George Nymph
Cream Midge *Dixella* spp.	March–April	Midday	20-24	Light Cahill	Light Cahill Nymph

Late Spring Hatches and Matches for Aquatic Insects (May/June)

Common & Latin Names	Emergence Days	Time of Day	Hook Size	Matching Dry Patterns	Matching Nymph/ Wet Patterns
Gray Fox *Stenonema fuscum*	May/June	Mid- to late afternoon	14-16	Gray Fox Ginger Quill Gray Fox Variant	Muskrat Beadhead Hare's Ear
Green Drake *Ephemera guttulata*	May	Late afternoon to evening	8-12	Green Drake Paradrake White Wulff Coffin Fly	Green Drake Nymph My Pet Beadhead Green Nymph Eastern Green Drake Nymph
March Brown *Maccaffertium vicarium* *(Stenonema vicarium)*	Early May	Midday	12-16	March Brown Royal Wulff Ausable Wulff	Beadhead Hare's Ear March Brown Nymph Beadhead Hare's Ear March Brown Nymph Beadhead Pheasant Yallarhammar
Light Cahill *Stenonema ithaca*	May/June	Afternoon to late evening	14-16	Light Cahill Hazel Creek Jim Charley	Light Cahill Nymph Yallarhammar
Sulphur Mayfly *Ephemerella dorothea*	May/June	Late afternoon to evening	16-18	Sulphur Light Cahill Hazel Creek Jim Charley	Yallarhammar Dark Sulphur Nymph Tellico Nymph
Maroon Drake *Isonychia sadleri*	May	Late afternoon (sporadic)	8-10	Red Quill	Yallarhammar My Pet
Mahogany Dun (or Leadwing Coachman, or Slate Drake) *Isonychia bicolor*	June	All day (sporadic)	12	Adams Royal Coachman	My Pet Hare's Ear
Rusty Spinners *Baetis tricaudatus*	May/June	Afternoon to evening	14-16	Rusty Wulff Orange Palmer Humpy	Yallarhammar Tellico Nymph Secret Weapon
Tiny Blue-Winged Olives *Attenella attenuate*	Late May–June	Early and late afternoon	18-22	BWO Standard BWO Parachute	Beadhead My Pet Beadhead Pheasant
Gray Drake *Siphlonurus occidentalis*	June	Late afternoon to evening	12-16	Gray Wulff Adams	Beadhead My Pet
Green/Apple Green Caddis *Rhyacophila* spp.	May	Mid- to late morning	14-18	Greenbrier Special Olive Caddis	Yallarhammar Chartreuse Caddis Green-Tied Tellico Secret Weapon
Mottled Green Caddis *Rhyacophila atrata*	Late May–June	Mid- to late morning	14-18	Greenbrier Special Olive Caddis Female Caddis	Green Streaker Yallarhammar Goddard Nymph

(continued on page 90)

Late Spring Hatches and Matches for Aquatic Insects (May/June) (continued)

Common & Latin Names	Emergence Days	Time of Day	Hook Size	Matching Dry Patterns	Matching Nymph/ Wet Patterns
Yellow Caddis *Chimarra aterrima*	Late June	Mid- to late morning	14-18	Yellow Caddis Goddard Caddis	Beadhead Prince Sparse Yallarhammar Tellico Nymph
Black Caddis *Chimarra aterrima*	May–early June (at higher elevations)	Midday to late evening	14-16	Dark Elk Wing Humpy Forky Tail Crow	Beadhead George Nymph
Short-Horned Sedge Caddis *Glossosoma intermedium*	May/June	Morning and evening	18-22	Goddard Caddis Tan Pale Green Caddis	Beadhead My Pet
Cinnamon Caddis *Ceratopsyche slossonae*	June	Mid- to late morning (mainly Abrams)	16-18	Dark Brown Elk Wing Cinnamon Caddis Adult	Yallarhammar
Little Sister Caddis (Little Olive Sledge) *Cheumatopsyche* spp.	June	Early morning to late afternoon (mainly Abrams)	18	Elk Hair Caddis Pickett Fence Deer Hair Caddis	Beadhead Solomon's Goddard Pupa Tellico Nymph
Little Yellow Stonefly (or Tawny Stonefly) *Isoperla bilineata*	May–June	Midday	12-16	Bucktail Caddis Yellow Palmer Yellow Sally Stimulator Elk Wing Caddis Greenbrier Special Little Yellow Stone Giant Black Stone	Yallarhammar Yellow Stonefly Nymph
Giant Black Stonefly *Pteronarcys scotti*	May–June	Early morning	12-14	Giant Black Stone	Montana Nymph George Nymph Crow Nymph Black Stonefly Nymph
Brown Stonefly *Isoperla bilineata*	May–June	Midday	14-16	Deer Hair Caddis Pickett Fence Little Brown Stone Dark Elk Wing Caddis	Forky Tail Crow Dark Stone Brown Stone Soft Hackles
Golden Stonefly *Acroneuria carolinensis*	Late May–June	Midday	14-16	Yellow Palmer Chuck Caddis	Golden Nugget Golden Stonefly Nymph
Olive Midge *Dixella* spp.	May	Midday	18-20	Adams Variant Griffith's Gnat	Hare's Ear
Cream Midge *Dixella* spp.	May/June	Midday	20-24	Light Cahill	Light Cahill Nymph

Summer Hatches and Matches for Aquatic Insects (July/August)

Common & Latin Names	Emergence Days	Time of Day	Hook Size	Matching Dry Patterns	Matching Nymph/ Wet Patterns
Gray Fox *Stenonema fuscum*	Early July (higher elevations)	Mid- to late afternoon	16	Gray Fox Ginger Quill Gray Fox Variant	Beadhead Hare's Ear Muskrat
Light Cahill *Stenonema ithaca*	Early July (higher elevations)	Late afternoon to evening	16	Light Cahill Hazel Creek Jim Charley	Light Cahill Nymph
Sulphur Mayfly *Ephemerella dorothea*	Early July (higher elevations)	Late afternoon to evening	16-18	Sulphur Light Cahill Hazel Creek Jim Charley	Yallarhammar Dark Sulphur Nymph
Mahogany Dun (or Slate Drake, or Leadwing Coachman) *Isonychia bicolor*	August	All day (sporadic)	12	Adams Thunderhead	Beadhead Hare's Ear Leadwing Coachman
Black Quill *Leptophlebia johnsoni*	July–early August (higher elevations)	Late evening	14	Gray Fox	Forky Tail Crow Secret Weapon
Rusty Spinners *Baetis tricaudatus*	July	Afternoon and evening	14-16	Rusty Wulff Orange Palmer	Yallarhammar Tellico Nymph
Tiny Blue-Winged Olives *Attenella attenuate*	July–August	Early morning and late afternoon	18-22	BWO Standard BWO Parachute	Beadhead Pheasant Beadhead Hare's Ear
Gray Drake *Siphlonurus occidentalis*	July	Late afternoon to evening	12-16	Gray Wulff Adams	Beadhead My Pet
Yellow Quill *Heptagenia julia*	August	Late evening	14-16	Quill Paradun Gray-Winged Yellow Quill	Yallarhammar
Gray-Brown Caddis *Brachycentrus americanus*	July–August	Late afternoon to dark	14-18	Dark Elk Wing Chuck Caddis	Gray Brown Pupa Brown Caddis Pupa
Mottled Green Caddis *Rhyacophila atrata*	July–August	Mid- to late morning	14-18	Greenbrier Special Olive Caddis	Green Streaker Yallarhammar Goddard Nymph
Yellow Caddis *Hydropsyche carolina*	July–early August	Mid- to late morning	14-18	Yellow Caddis	Beadhead Prince Sparse Yallarhammar Tellico Nymph
Tan Caddis *Heteroplectron americanus*	July–August	Mid- to late morning	14-18	Tan Caddis Caribou Caddis	Stickbait Tan Caddis Pupa

(continued on page 92)

Summer Hatches and Matches for Aquatic Insects (July/August) (continued)

Common & Latin Names	Emergence Days	Time of Day	Hook Size	Matching Dry Patterns	Matching Nymph/ Wet Patterns
Black Caddis *Chimarra aterrima*	July–August	Midday to late evening (at higher elevations)	14-16	Dark Elk Wing	Black Tellico Nymph
Short-Horned Sedge (or Short-Horned Caddis) *Glossosoma intermedium*	July–early August	Morning and evening	18-22	Goddard Caddis Tan Pale Green Caddis	Beadhead My Pet
Cinnamon Caddis *Ceratopsyche slossonae*	Mid-July (mainly Abrams)	Mid- to late morning	16-18	Dark Brown Elk Wing Cinnamon Caddis Adult	Yallarhammar
Little Sister Caddis (Little Olive Sledge) *Cheumatopsyche* spp.	Early July (mainly Abrams)	Early morning to late afternoon	18	Elk Hair Caddis Pickett Fence Deer Hair Caddis	Beadhead Solomon's Yallarhammar Goddard's Pupa
Little Green Stonefly *Suwallia marginata*	July–early August	Early morning	16	Clark's Stonefly Green Stimulator Little Green Stonefly Madame X Greer	Madame X Sofa Pillow Stimulator Kaufmann's Stonefly
Little Yellow Stonefly (or Tawny Stonefly) *Isoperla bilineata*	July–August	Midday	12-16	Bucktail Caddis Yellow Palmer Pickett Fence Elk Wing Caddis Greenbrier Special Little Yellow Stone Yellow Sally Jim Charley	Yallarhammar Yellow Stonefly Nymph
Brown Stonefly *Isoperla bilineata*	July	Midday	14-16	Deer Hair Caddis Pickett Fence Little Brown Stone Dark Elkwing Caddis	Forky Tail Crow Dark Stone Brown Stone
Golden Stonefly *Acroneuria carolinensis*	July–August	Midday	14-16	Yellow Palmer Chuck Caddis	Golden Nugget Golden Stonefly Nymph Bitch Creek
Little Yellow Summer Stone (or Roach Flies) *Acroneuria carolinensis*	July–August	Midday	14-16	Little Yellow Sally Madame X Edwards Yellow Stonefly Jim Charley	Yallarhammar Little Sally Nymph Secret Weapon
Little Brown Needle Stonefly *Paraleuctra sara*	Late August	All day	18	Dark Elk Wing Caddis Little Brown Needle Stonefly	Beadhead My Pet
Cream Midge *Dixella* spp.	July–August	Midday	20-24	Light Cahill	Light Cahill Nymph

Autumn Hatches and Matches for Aquatic Insects (September/October)

Common & Latin Names	Emergence Days	Time of Day	Hook Size	Matching Dry Patterns	Matching Nymph/ Wet Patterns
Light Cahill *Stenonema ithaca*	Early September (higher elevations)	Afternoon to late evening	16	Light Cahill Hazel Creek Jim Charley	Light Cahill Nymph
Mahogany Dun (or Slate Drake, or Leadwing Coachman) *Isonychia bicolor*	September	All day (sporadic)	12	Adams Thunderhead	Beadhead Hare's Ear Leadwing Coachman
Little Yellow Quill *Leucrocuta hebe*	September– October	Late evening	14-16	Quill Paradun Winged Yellow Quill	Yallarhammar
Rusty Spinners *Baetis tricaudatus*	Early September (higher elevations)	Afternoon and evening	14-16	Rusty Wulff Orange Palmer	Yallarhammar Tellico Nymph
Tiny Blue-Winged Olives *Attenella attenuate*	September– October	Early morning and late afternoon	18-22	BWO Standard BWO Parachute	Beadhead Pheasant Beadhead Hare's Ear
Gray Drake *Siphlonurus occidentalis*	September– October	Late afternoon to evening	12-16	Gray Wulff Adams	Beadhead My Pet
Gray-Brown Caddis *Brachycentrus americanus*	September	Late afternoon to dark	14-18	Dark Elk Wing Chuck Caddis	Gray Caddis Pupa Dark Caddis Pupa Copper Caddis Pupa Brown
Yellow Caddis *Hydropsyche carolina*	September– October	Mid- to late morning	14-18	Yellow Caddis	Beadhead Prince Sparse Yallarhammar Tellico Nymph
Tan Caddis *Heteroplectron americanus*	September– October	Mid- to late morning	14-18	Tan Caddis Caribou Caddis	Stickbait Tan Caddis Pupa
Black Caddis *Chimarra aterrima*	September	Midday to late evening (at higher elevations)	14-16	Dark Elk Wing	Black Tellico Nymph
Great Brown Autumn Sedge *Pycnopsyche* spp.	September– October	All day	14	Dark Elk Wing	Dark Caddis Pupa Copper Caddis Pupa Brown
Short-Horned Sedge (or Short-Horned Caddis) *Glossosoma intermedium*	September– October	Morning and evening	18-22	Goddard Caddis Tan Pale Green Caddis	Beadhead My Pet

(continued on page 94)

Autumn Hatches and Matches for Aquatic Insects (September/October) (continued)

Common & Latin Names	Emergence Days	Time of Day	Hook Size	Matching Dry Patterns	Matching Nymph/ Wet Patterns
Little Yellow Stonefly (or Tawny Stonefly) *Isoperla bilineata*	September– October	Midday	12-16	Bucktail Caddis Yellow Palmer Jim Charley Elk Wing Caddis Greenbrier Special Lil' Yellow Stone Yellow Sally	Yallarhammar Yellow Stonefly Nymph
Little Yellow Summer Stone (or Roach Flies) Peltoperlidae *Acroneuria carolinensis*	September– October	Midday	14-16	Little Yellow Sally Madame X Edwards Yellow Stonefly	Yallarhammar Little Sally Nymph
Little Brown Needle Stonefly *Paraleuctra sara*	September	All day	18	Dark Elk Wing Caddis Little Brown Needle Stonefly	Beadhead My Pet
Cream Midge *Dixella* spp.	September– October	Midday	20-24	Light Cahill	Light Cahill Nymph

Early Winter Hatches and Matches for Aquatic Insects (November/December)

Common & Latin Names	Emergence Days	Time of Day	Hook Size	Matching Dry Patterns	Matching Nymph/ Wet Patterns
Mahogany Dun (or Slate Drake, or Leadwing Coachman) *Isonychia bicolor*	To mid- November	All day (sporadic)	12	Adams Thunderhead	Beadhead Hare's Ear Leadwing Coachman
Little Yellow Quill *Leucrocuta hebe*	To mid- December	Afternoon	14-16	Quill Paradun Gray-Winged Yellow Quill	Yallarhammar
Tiny Blue-Winged Olives *Attenella attenuate*	November– December	Early morning and late afternoon	18-22	BWO Standard BWO Parachute	Beadhead Pheasant Beadhead Hare's Ear
Yellow Caddis *Hydropsyche carolina*	November- December	Mid- to late morning	14-18	Yellow Caddis	Beadhead Prince Sparse Yallarhammar Tellico Nymph
Little Brown Needle *Paraleuctra sara*	November– December	All day	18	Dark Elk Wing Caddis Little Brown Needle Stonefly	Beadhead My Pet
Olive Midge *Dixella* spp.	November– December	Midday	18-20	Adams Variant Griffith's Gnat	Hare's Ear

CHAPTER NINE

Terrestrial Insects of the Great Smoky Mountains

You could argue that the grasshopper is king of the terrestrials in the Smokies. JAY NICHOLS

There may not be a place in the world where terrestrial insects play a bigger role in the diet of trout than in the streams of the Great Smoky Mountains National Park. This is true for a number of reasons, not the least of which is that trout rely on them for nourishment for almost three full months out of the year. Frequent heavy rainfall makes these land-bound insects regularly available to trout, and the fish have come to depend on them tremendously. Beginning in the spring and through the summer months, and especially during autumn, land-dwelling insects are vitally important sources of food for these fish.

The diversity of the terrestrial insects washed into a stream is, like everything else in the Great Smoky Mountains, surpassed only by the diversity of macroinvertebrates of the Amazon. As many as 7,000 species are known to occur here, and it is estimated that another 10,000 possibly live here. There are 108 species of ants among the many terrestrial insects found in abundance here, and at least 45 species belonging to the Orthoptera suborder Caelifera (grasshoppers, grouse locusts, and pygmy mole crickets) make their homes here as well. If you consider beetles, leaf beetles alone number over 330 species, all of which probably get washed into a stream at the same time when there is a big thunderstorm in late August.

When the feeding attention of trout and bass is keyed on terrestrial insects, it is a magical time for fly fishermen. Rarely are these streams more productive than when these fish are taking grasshoppers, ants, and other terrestrials during the summer. Granted, most of the time these waters are low and clear, which does little to help the efforts of the average angler. However, you'll typically find great fishing early in the morning, late in the evening, on rainy days, or on days directly following a rainstorm. Understanding what foods are most available to stream trout during this time is the secret to catching these fish during the hot-weather months as well as most of autumn.

Between midsummer and late autumn the trout in these streams rely less on aquatic insects than at any other time of year. This is for two reasons. One is that the cyclic unavailability of aquatic insects coincides with the abundance of terrestrials during the summer. The other is the seasonal abundance of terrestrial insects that find their way into these streams. Beginning in early spring, hatches of may-, stone-, and caddisflies dominate trout feeding efforts. Members of these orders deposit most of their eggs in the streams between March and June to replenish their populations. It is not until late autumn that these hatch and become significant sources of food for what anglers refer to as "catchable-size trout."

Terrestrials become available to stream trout in a variety of ways: they can simply jump into the water, as is often the case of a grasshopper, or they can fall from limbs and other greenery hanging over the water, as is the case with caterpillars and jassids. Other terrestrial insects that can fly, such as bees, Japanese beetles, and locusts, also often find their way onto the surface of a stream. Generally, frequent late-summer and early autumn rains wash a bounty of terrestrial insects into the water. At this

Although their abundance varies from year to year, the Japanese beetle is often important to trout. JAY NICHOLS

time buggy, nondescript terrestrial fly patterns, such as the Woolly Worm, are deadly on these trout and bass.

Terrestrial insects provide easily seized, high-quality food at a time when the fish might otherwise have to expend considerable effort chasing minnows or crayfish. There are few terrestrial insects stream trout will not gulp down with gusto, especially on medium-size to small streams where land critters play a key role in the daily diets of trout.

One of the most interesting things about terrestrial insects fly fishermen should understand is that even when dead, these insects always float. This was first pointed out to me in the 1970s by Gerald Almy, then a staff writer for *Sports Afield*. Gerry also wrote the well-known book, *Tying and Fishing Terrestrials*. I took him on his first fishing trip to the Smokies, a bright early-morning jaunt to the falls at Abrams. He keeps telling me that he will eventually forgive me for that little outing, when I showed up with a significant supply of locally produced moonshine.

According to Gerry, nature prevents terrestrials from soaking up water when they are alive by providing them with nonporous bodies overlaid with wax. Essentially, terrestrials are waterproof. This is not to say a trout won't nab a grasshopper you offer on a line weighted down with a split shot sinker. However, it is a fact that a trout is more accustomed to taking a hopper from the surface than beneath it.

Grasshoppers are to Smoky Mountain trout what a rib eye steak is to you or me: a tasty, substantial mouthful that comes around too infrequently to pass up. Grasshoppers certainly are not the only major terrestrial that stream trout feed on, but in many instances they are of primary concern to anglers. When grasshoppers are available in large quantities, trout watch for these rib eyes on the surface. Anyone who has ever found themselves on a quality trout stream armed with a few good grasshopper imitations at a time when these terrestrials are numerous knows what it's like to experience a little bit of heaven on earth.

Another terrestrial insect these trout often key on is the jassid, or leafhopper. Related to grasshoppers but much smaller, jassids commonly live in streamside grasses and other greenery. When you're fishing streams where you see trout dimpling the surface along the extreme edge of the water, odds are these fish are munching down jassids, although occasionally this will happen when wood ants are working near the water.

At this time of the season, stream trout must keep a sharp eye out for any possible source of food. Several summers ago, while fishing Panther Creek, I came upon a spot where a basketball-size hornet's nest hung over the tail of a pool. Apparently the hornets were cleaning house, as enough debris was hitting the water to attract three footlong trout. Tying on a bee pattern dry fly, I caught two of the trout before the third wised up and left.

Late-summer and early-autumn trout depend on terrestrial insects to varying degrees. At food-rich streams such as Abrams Creek where streamborne food is always available in large quantities, terrestrial patterns are often outproduced by patterns such as the Adams. However, in the most classic freestone streams of the park, terrestrials are vital sources of nutrition.

There are many seasonal terrestrials that are easy to overlook. For example, when the sourwood worms are available in early summer, trout relish these whitish-colored morsels. The thin, bright green inchworms we often see suspended from trees are another often-overlooked, but highly sought-after tidbit. When they are common, Japanese beetles can be imitated with great success. During summer and autumn, it is usually a big mistake not to have a supply of terrestrial fly patterns with you.

Fly fishermen who have not discovered the effectiveness of late-summer and early-autumn terrestrial patterns will be astounded when trying these offerings. Fly catalogs boast many patterns designed to mimic grasshoppers, jassids, ants, beetles, grubs, and more. Grasshopper patterns are my personal favorite, with the old reliable Joe's Hopper being tough to top. Should you find yourself astream without a hopper pattern when you need one, you can push a Muddler Minnow into service. Dressed with a floatant, a Muddler Minnow is a pretty good grasshopper imitation. Frankly there are a couple dozen hopper patterns that will work, each one just about as good as another.

When fly fishing for trout in late summer and early autumn, ant patterns are also worth trying—they are the unsung heroes during this season. Periodically

Ants are one of the most consistent terrestrial sources of food for trout in the Smokies.
JAY NICHOLS

examine the contents of the stomachs of the trout you catch—if they are feeding heavily on grasshoppers, the stiff legs of these creatures will be easily seen when the stomach is split. Ants, on the other hand, are not so easily discerned. Sometimes you will find complete or partial bodies of ants, but most of the time you'll only see a blackish, or sometimes reddish, blob in the stomach.

At this time of year ants are extremely common along trout streams. Although ants are small, trout will always seize them when they're available. You should always carry ant patterns in black and red, sizes 10- 18, when fly fishing for trout during late summer and early autumn. My best results have occurred when concentrating only on the edges of streams, but trout will take ant patterns just about anywhere they are offered during this time of year.

Fish ant patterns, and just about all other terrestrial insect patterns, in much the same way you would present dry-fly patterns. Exceptions are when fly fishing along grassy edges, where many terrestrial insects typically fall into streams. Under these circumstances, adding a bit of action to the fly often makes terrestrial patterns irresistible to fish. Fantastic fly fishing is often available along shallow runs by offering terrestrial fly patterns such as a leafhopper or Japanese beetle within a foot or less of the streambank.

One of the best things about fly fishing using terrestrial patterns is that you do not have to be there when a hatch comes off. You don't even have to get up early to

Food-conscious big brown trout are especially vulnerable to big terrestrial patterns like beetles and hoppers. LOUIS CAHILL

get in on prime fishing. The warmer it gets, the more active many species of terrestrial insects become. High-noon fishing can often be high-octane fishing, if stream flow levels are in your favor. You'll be pleasantly surprised if you have not yet discovered how well terrestrial insect patterns can increase your catches of stream trout during late summer and early autumn. Trout that have grown large since spring are there for the taking.

Late-summer and autumn fly boxes should have at least half of the following:
Green Hopper (sizes 10-14)
Brown/Amber Hopper (sizes 8-12)
Little River Ant (sizes 12-18)
Cinnamon Ant (sizes 12-18)
Green Inchworm (sizes 10-14)
Japanese Beetle (sizes 12-14)
Wood Bee (sizes 10-14)
Yellowjacket (sizes 8-12)
Black Beetle (sizes 12-16)
Loco Beetle (sizes 12-16)
Hi-Viz Ant (sizes 14-18)

CHAPTER TEN

Streamers: The Forgotten "Flies"

If you want big trout, come armed with streamers. LOUIS CAHILL

W hen I can catch trout on dry flies, that's what I cast. My second choice is to fish with nymphs. If that also fails, my next choice is a streamer. Streamers represent minnows, baitfish, leeches, crayfish, and other creatures, all of which have the ability to swim through the water and are preyed upon by trout. It isn't that I don't like to fish streamers unless I need to. In fact, I have fished streamers and wet flies most of my life, and they saved many days for me in the Great Smoky Mountains National Park. I just prefer the simplicity of dry-fly fishing to streamer fishing and all of the extra effort involved.

The streams of the Great Smoky Mountains are incredibly diverse in terms of the number of critters that reside there with the trout and bass. These streams are home to nearly sixty species of fish in twelve different families, including lampreys, darters, shiners, minnows, suckers, bass, and trout. There are four federally protected fish species in the park, all of which live in lower Abrams Creek: the spotfin chub (listed as threatened), duskytail darter (endangered), smoky madtom (endangered), and yellowfin madtom (threatened). Efforts are underway to reintroduce these fish back into Abrams Creek and some signs of success have been noted.

For those who like numbers, darters are the most numerous of the minnows, numbering over a dozen different species. Nine species of shiners occur here, followed by four members of the dace clan, and as many chubs. These waters sport two species of sculpins, two species of lamprey, and a smattering of other little fish with names such as brook silverside, fatlips minnow, fathead minnow, and western mosquitofish. All of these plus the fry of bigger fish, such as several members of the redhorse and sunfish clans, are all potential meals for trout and bass on any day of the year.

When it comes to using streamers in the park there is considerable truth in the old adage that bigger flies take bigger fish. However, it is also true that there are times when a streamer will take trout on these waters when nothing else will work. Weather can dramatically impact these trout streams. Over the years I have often traveled to a stream to discover it was too high and roily for dry-fly fishing. Streamers worked slowly and sometimes aggressively in murky, high water have often netted me surprising results, especially at the lower end of big streams such as the Hazel and Little River.

I have not had as much success with streamers on bright sunny days. Early morning and late evening, when the sun is off the water, are better because trout don't like to move from their resting positions as much when the sun is high. I have had some of my best success with streamers on heavily overcast days, especially when it is cool and windy. An exception to this is during the summer following a thundershower that puts color into a stream and increases its volume. This is perhaps the number-one time to catch a big brown at many of the streams in the Great Smoky Mountains.

Over five dozen different species of fish serve as food for trout in these waters. WILLIAM
MCLEMORE

There are two basic types of streamer patterns: imitators and attractors. Imitators represent a specific type of food that is preyed upon by the trout. Fishing imitator patterns requires knowledge of each food form and how it behaves. Attractors don't represent anything in particular, but are designed to excite a trout into striking. Attractors are usually brightly colored and may contain mylar or other highly reflective materials.

Forage fish common to the Great Smoky Mountains can be separated into free-swimming and bottom-dwelling types. The free swimmers include juvenile trout, darters, suckers, chubs, and dace. Sculpins make up the majority of bottom-dwelling forage fish of interest to fly fishermen here. Free-swimming fish are found in areas where they hold against the current much the same as trout. From here they feed on small aquatic and terrestrial insects. Under most circumstances these gifted speedsters are very difficult for trout to catch.

Free swimmers are homebodies that rarely venture far from shelter and quickly dart at high speed for cover when pursued by trout. Typically they can coexist with trout, who appear to be completely nonchalant until one of the smaller fish makes an erratic move or displays a slight hesitance. It is astonishing how quickly a darter will disappear the instant a trout sees it start to act differently than the other minnows.

Although it has only happened to me once, it is not uncommon to hook a small trout in these waters and watch a much larger trout charge after it while you retrieve it. I am convinced that it is the struggle of the smaller fish to free itself from the hook that triggers such predatory responses from the big fellows. Large trout quickly make a meal of any forage fish that is crippled or injured. Fishing a streamer with an erratic retrieve to represent a crippled minnow or fishing it dead drifted through a deep run is a deadly technique for hooking a big brown trout.

Occasionally when fishing the larger streams, observant fly fishermen get an opportunity to actually see trout rushing after baitfish. Trout will rush through the school, smashing into the small fish in an effort to disable them. They usually make several passes, returning to pick off the crippled survivors of the initial attack. I have seen this a couple of times when the hornyhead chubs are fluttering during the spring.

The accepted dogma of streamer fishing is that free-swimming imitations should be tied in the color and shape of the forage fish common to the stream. In

Generally, the more difficult the weather is, more productive a stream will be. LOUIS CAHILL

these waters, that covers a rainbow of colors and a variety of sizes. Many of these fish are silvery and patterns should include a little flash. Sparse patterns usually outperform heavily dressed streamers on flat water. However, the baitfish that seem to entice the most strikes in these streams are rather drab in color, with olives, tans, and browns usually outproducing the brightly hued, pretty stuff.

Admittedly there are times when a bright attractor streamer will outperform an exact imitation. All trout are territorial and will defend their territory when it is invaded by an intruder. This territory might be an undercut bank where a large brown trout is hiding, or it could be a feeding zone that a big fish has staked out to feed at his leisure. A bright, flashy streamer can excite a trout into striking when it appears to threaten its territory. Two of my favorites for this are the Zonker and the Clouser Minnow. Sometimes bright, flashy things entice strikes when exact imitations are ignored. Perhaps it is simple curiosity on the part of the trout.

I am of the opinion that the most important aspect of fishing a streamer is to mimic a baitfish seeking to escape a charging trout. Small fish instinctively know that they can't swim upstream against the current, and escape by racing for cover. When caught in the open, they flee at top speed, often leaping free of the water to avoid ingestion. Always strive to present a streamer broadside to a trout. All streamers look almost alike when viewed from directly behind. The most common presentation is to cast a streamer across and down and then strip it back in a steady motion—this is better than a series of fast bursts and pauses. This causes the fly to behave opposite from baitfish by swimming against the current. Avoid the temptation to put too much action on a streamer. Slow strips with a light flick of the tip of a fly rod imparts sufficient action to most streamers.

One of the best ways to take trout from the many deep pools of the Great Smoky Mountains is to cast upstream and retrieve the fly back down. Retrieve your streamer slightly faster than the current with flicks and strips so the fly darts ahead and starts to dive toward the bottom when it pauses. Trout skulking in the depths of pools will often charge downstream to attack streamers fished in this way. The downstream retrieve is an effective method for sculpin or crayfish imitations, which should be fished near the bottom.

The brown trout of the Great Smoky Mountains become surprisingly territorial when spawning time approaches in late autumn. Their spawning instincts urge these otherwise retiring predators to defend their territory from all comers, especially other brown trout. Once on the spawning redds, when opportunities arise small male brown trout rush in to fertilize the eggs. Many anglers discourage fishing in areas of active spawning. However, brown trout in park waters become aggressive weeks before spawning, especially those that run upstream from Fontana Lake. It is perfectly legal to fish for them in the streams of the national park.

Streamer Patterns for the Great Smoky Mountains (sizes 4 to 10)

Muddler Minnow	Chinos
Black-Nose Dace	Black Matuka
Hot Bead Bugger	Brook Trout Clouser
Woolly Bugger	Green Weenie
Black Ghost	Hornberg Muddler Streamer
Conehead Madonna	Spuddler
Carrie's Favorite	Mickey Finn
Bloody Zonker	Near 'Nuff Dumbbell Sculpin
Clouserish	Marabou Shiner
Clouser Deep Minnow	Baby Rainbow Trout
Zoo Cougar	

From top to bottom: Conehead Muddler, Clouser's Yellow/Olive Barred Mad Tom, Perfect Minnow Chartreuse/White, D's Hoover Mover, Sculpin Diving Minnow. JAY NICHOLS

CHAPTER ELEVEN

Fly Patterns

The brook trout in the Great Smoky Mountains are living reminders of the last Ice Age. LOUIS CAHILL

I n a very real sense, compiling the fly-tying recipes was the most difficult part of completing this book. Perusing the list, you will readily see that there is little in the way of rhyme or reason, at least in terms of strict guidelines of what patterns might qualify for inclusion. I've listed mostly what I refer to as old-time, traditional Great Smoky Mountains fly patterns that more or less originated in and around the national park. However, patterns with long histories on these waters, but that did not originate here—such as Montana Nymph—are also listed as it was my personal determination that they are "part of the story."

You will also find the cursory inclusion of old-time patterns such as Pink Lady, Wickham's Fancy, and Cowdung. This is done for the sake of completeness and to acknowledge that these patterns were among the very first cast on the waters of the Great Smoky Mountains. One of my goals for this book was to gather as much material as I could to give readers the most comprehensive experience possible. I've also added a smattering of newer patterns that are just too effective on these waters for me not to talk about just a little.

It is not an oversight that I've pretty much ignored patterns pertaining to midges and other itty-bitty bugs. One reason is that I can barely see the damn things and as such have little interest in them. The other is that the current high level of interest in midges, scuds, and sow bugs is largely among those fly casting at tailwater rivers. These insects and the patterns tied to mimic them are literally of another world that is largely apart from the waters of the Great Smoky Mountains.

I've given much the same treatment to streamers, which I do like to tie and fish in the waters of the Great Smoky Mountains. However, with few exceptions, streamers used on these waters differ little from the streamers used in other places. This is not a categorical statement though, and though I do believe streamer fishing is making a big comeback among the fly fishermen of the region, it was my decision to limit the list of patterns. I am sure a few of them will raise eyebrows, and my greatest worry is that I've overlooked patterns.

Smoky Mountain Candy

As a kid we used to go to Gatlinburg to watch the toffee-making shops work goat-sized globs of emulsified sugar into what we called Smoky Mountain candy. It was irresistible. A dry-fly pattern developed by east Tennessee fly-tying legend Walter Babb of Sweetwater, Smoky Mountain Candy is irresistible to trout. Curious about the secret power of Babb's pattern, I held one in my mouth to see if it was sweet. It was not. (If you try this yourself, my advice is to use a barbless hook. My trip to the emergency room to have the hook removed from my tongue was a bit embarrassing to my wife.)

Hook: #10-14 Tiemco 881S
Thread: Brown 6/0 Danville
Wing: Brown calf tail or body hair
Tail: Moose body hair
Body: Dirty yellow fur (⅓ yellow, ⅓ tan, ⅓ tawny)
Hackle: Brown and grizzly mixed

The Sheep Fly

The Sheep Fly was created in 1950 by Newland Saunders of Caldwell County, NC, who recently passed away. According to Bill Everhardt, Newland's mentor and fishing partner, several decades ago during an autumn fishing trip, Newland was being pestered by a fearless hornet. Swatting at the hornet, Newland dropped his fly box, freeing one of his Sheep Flies in the process. Diving to the ground, the hornet snatched up Newland's Sheep Fly and flew off with it to its nest.

The Sheep Fly is a fantastic imitation of the biting, bloodthirsty deerflies of summer and fall. Sometimes called small horse flies, deerflies are particularly prevalent along densely wooded streams in these mountains. The Sheep Fly has a still-growing reputation as a big trout taker, and was heralded by Cap Weise of Lenior, NC, who espoused the virtues of the pattern.

Hook:	#8-14 Mustad 9671 or Mustad 79380
Thread:	Black 6/0
Tail:	Brown saddle hackle
Body:	Muskrat fur with guard hairs
Beard:	Brown saddle hackle
Wings:	Grizzly hackle tips
Head:	Peacock herl
Weight:	Fine .010" to .030" wire

Streaker Nymph

The late, great outdoor writer Byron W. Dalrymple introduced me to the Streaker Nymph, a great caddis pupae imitation, which he told me was better for catching trout than Merita bread on a hook. Dalrymple, a Texan better known for writing deer-hunting books in the 1970s, died a few years ago. It was not until shortly before his death that I learned the origins of the Streaker Nymph's name. It was so christened in the early 1970s, during the streaking craze on the country's college campuses, because the body of the original was stripped down to nothing other than tightly pulled latex harvested from hospital gloves. Prominently noted in L .J. DeCuir's *Southeastern Flies*, DeCuir refers to it as a "skinny Tellico-like nymph" believed to have been created to imitate stickbait.

Hook: #10-16 Mustad 9671
Thread: Yellow 6/0
Body: Latex
Beard: Ginger saddle hackle
Head: White hackle
Weight: Fine .005" to .010" wire

The Backscratch

An oldie that is likely a variation of the Brown Hackle fly used by old timers at these waters a century ago, the Backscratch can be used to match various nymphal forms of stoneflies or mayflies found in the waters of the Great Smoky Mountains and other freestone trout streams from northern Virginia to Georgia. Graced with an intriguing name, one cannot help but wonder if the Backscratch is somehow indicative of it being some sort of angling panacea for when you need a fly to land in just the "right spot" beside a low-hanging laurel leaf. You know the feeling . . .

Hook: #12-14 Tiemco 100
Thread: Red 3/0 Danville Monocord
Body: Peacock
Hackle: Brown saddle
Tail: Goose biot

Royal Coachman Dry

A purely Yankee pattern embraced by fly fishermen of the region, the Royal Coachman, despite its name, is but a commoner. Quoting from *Favorite Flies and Their Histories* by Mary Orvis Marbury, "The Royal Coachman was first made in 1878 by John Hailey, a professional fly-dresser living in New York City." The red floss body was developed to strengthen an older pattern called the Coachman. This was done because the teeth of the brook trout were too hard on the Standard Coachman. As the story goes, it was labeled "Royal," as it reminded people of the British redcoats. This name was suggested by Charles Orvis's brother. Charles Orvis went on to found the famous fly-fishing company that bears his name. This is the original John Hailey pattern. Variations are infinite, including Benny Joe Craig's use of the red plastic strip from packs of Lucky Strike cigarettes for the body band of his Royal Coachman patterns tied before World War II.

Hook: #6-14 Mustad 3906
Thread: Black silk, monocord, or nylon
Tag: Gold
Tail: Green-barred wood duck feathers
Body: Peacock herl with scarlet floss center
Wing: White goose biot
Hackle: Brown cock

Smoky Mountain Forktail Dry

When I wrote my first guidebook to fishing in the Great Smoky Mountains, notations of the Smoky Mountain Forky Tail resulted in a bit of confusion with the SM Forktail, a dry-fly pattern. Had I included a picture of the former in those early editions, doubtless this would not have happened as the two patterns are quite different. The SM Forktail is a dry stimulator-style pattern that works very well anywhere stoneflies are plentiful, which pretty much describes the Great Smoky Mountains. Roger Lowe refers to a pattern called the Orange Forked Tail that is very much like the SM Forktail, the major difference being that his tail is orange whereas mine is gray, brown, or olive. You can also substitute gray red fox underfur for the natural opossum suggested for the body. Some recipes call for duck wings instead of goose biots for the wing, tied in an up-and-out position.

Hook: #12-16 standard dry-fly hook
Thread: Black or gray silk
Tail: Goose biots crossed outward
Body: Natural opossum
Wing: Goose biots
Hackle: Grizzly and brown mix

Smoky Mountain Blackbird

The Smoky Mountain Blackbird is one of a group of soft-hackle flies used in the area for over a century. Kirk Jenkins of Newport, TN, introduced me to the pattern, which he said he learned from an old timer from the Cosby area. He tied the pattern using black hare's mask dubbing and hackle taken from the wings and tail of anything from a crow or starling to a red-winged blackbird or a grackle. Highly versatile, the Smoky Mountain Blackbird can be tied weighted or unweighted, and is sometimes tied with a small tungsten bead head.

Hook: #8-14 Mustad 9671 or Mustad 79380
Thread: Black 6/0
Body: Black hare's mask
Beard: Brown saddle hackle
Hackle: Split, cleaned, water-soaked wing or tail feathers of starling or blackbird

Yellow-Bellied Nymph

The Yellow-Bellied Nymph, cooked up by an unknown tier in the 1950s, is thought to have originated in the Robbinsville area. It is reminiscent of the Tellico Nymph and may very well be a variant of it. However, I wish more information were available on this dandy little trout-catching pattern. A note on the tail—bronze peacock herl works best.

Hook: #10-12 Mustad 3906B
Thread: Lemon yellow to match as closely as possible the color of the body material
Weight: Lead wire (.010")
Tail: Peacock herl
Body: Lemon-yellow wool matching color to thread
Legs: Peacock sword

Speck Wet

The Speck Wet, an interesting wet-fly pattern similar to the Deer Fly, has a long history on the North Carolina side of the national park. Joe Bishop of Lenoir City, TN, is credited with its invention. Walter Babb, one of the region's best-known tiers, favors the Speck Wet, and its popularity among local anglers is largely due to Babb. He not only espouses the Speck, but each year at fly-tying seminars also demonstrates how to create this productive pattern.

Hook: #10-14 Tiemco 3769
Thread: Black 6/0 UNI-Thread
Tail: Brown and grizzly hen hackles mixed
Body: Spun deer or caribou, trimmed Irresistible-style
Hackle: Brown and grizzly hen hackle fibers, mixed, two wraps each

Renegade

Locals have cast the Renegade in park waters for decades, perhaps as early as the mid-1940s. No one knows what this old pattern represents, but many can attest to its effectiveness. According to Ernest Hemingway, "Taylor Williams came to work in Sun Valley in 1937 [as a hunting and fishing guide]. He was an excellent dry fly fisherman. He always said that he was responsible for the Renegade fly" (*Heaven on Earth: Stories of Fly Fishing, Fun & Faith* by Andrew Marshall Wayment). You may feel like arguing with Hemingway, but I'll shut my mouth in deference to one of my heroes.

Hook: #10-18 Tiemco 100
Thread: Black 6/0 70-denier Danville
Aft Hackle: Brown cock
Fore Hackle: White cock
Body: Peacock herl

Light Cahill

Dan Cahill originated the Light Cahill, a sparsely dressed classic Catskill dry fly, over 120 years ago. Ray Bergman, author of the best-selling *Trout* (1938), said of the Light Cahill, "If it was necessary to confine my assortment of flies to only two or three, this would be one of them." Bergman added, "It is an eastern pattern, particularly effective in the Catskill waters and similar eastern mountain streams." Still, he recounted that it also served him well in Michigan, Wyoming, and California. The Light Cahill is a basic imitation of a Pale Morning Dun or a Pale Evening Dun, and is a must in every fly box carried in the Great Smoky Mountains.

Hook: #12-16 Mustad 94840 or Daiichi 1180
Thread: Pale yellow or white 8/0 (70 denier)
Tail: Cream or straw-colored hackle fibers
Body: Cream male red fox belly fur dubbing
Wing: Wood duck or mandarin duck flank feather
Hackle: Two cream or straw-colored cock hackles

Smoky Mountain Forky Tail Nymph

This pattern will "raise hackles" among some self-proclaimed southern fly-pattern specialists. Many of them do not understand the need for using the shortest, smaller feathers to give the pattern a "stickleback" appearance. Instead, they use longer feathers that impart a more "soft hackle" look. I am passing this pattern along the way I was taught by Kirk Jenkins, a Newport, TN, fly tier who passed away in the winter of 2012. Kirk was a close friend with whom I worked for over seventeen years at American Enka, in Lowland, TN. Once the largest manufacturer of fiber in the world, it was bought and operated by BASF before closing its doors in the 1990s.

Kirk gave me my first actual tying vise that had not been handcrafted by my father. I still always bought two flies from Kirk, even after I mastered creating oddities that caught trout: the Yallarhammar and Smoky Mountain Forky Tail Nymph. I was not blessed with much patience, and I never liked wrapping split feathers. I did enjoy crow shooting though, and I had developed a secret stare that I would inflict on flickers (a type of woodpecker) that made them fall over dead when I snapped my fingers. Kirk usually had plenty of crow feathers, but no fly tier has ever actually had enough flicker plumes. Our bartering arrangement worked well.

Kirk's Smoky Mountain Forky Tail Nymph, which he usually referred to as a "crow fly," is a deadly pattern. Back in the day, I used to fish them in tandem with Tellico Nymphs. I never kept count of how often it happened per day, but it wasn't all that uncommon to catch two trout at the same time. If you tie the Forky Tail Nymph correctly, with 1/16-inch split wing or tail feathers of a crow, it looks "prickly." Soak the wing in warm water after splitting to help make it more pliable and less likely to splinter. You don't generally trim Forky Tails, and they look like a stubby Yallarhammar.

Hook: #10-14 Mustad 9671
Thread: Black
Body: Ostrich herl
Rib: One side of a crow wing or tail feather
Hackle: Black saddle
Tail: Crow quill fibers
Weight: Lead wire (.010"), two wraps deep

Yallarhammar Series

Locals have cast versions of the Yallarhammer fly patterns in and around park waters for decades, perhaps as early as the mid-1800s. What does this classic pattern represent? In its oldest forms, it was a wet. I believe the collared version is older than the palmered version of the Yallarhammer, but that is mostly an educated guess. Modern tiers such as Kevin Howell, Walter Babb, Bill Everhardt, and Roger Lowe are largely responsible for the birth of the Yallarhammer series, which accounts for over a dozen or so distinct patterns.

There are a few tricks for tying with the wing and tail feathers from birds such as the Yellow Flicker woodpecker. The first thing to know is not to use plums from these state and federally protected birds. Wing feathers from grouse, starlings, dove, and quail dabbed in a solution of bleach and water look close enough to the plumes of a Yellow Flicker for tiers to create realistic-looking Yallarhammer flies.

Before attempting to tie with these feathers, you must prep them. Use a razor blade to split shafts of the feathers along their center. Next soak the split shafts in warm water fifteen or so minutes. Putting the quills into water softens them enough that they can be wrapped around a hook without cracking or breaking. After this, use the point of a large pin to clean out the remaining fiber inside of the divided shaft. If it is a thick feather and your hands are steady, trim away the excess portions of the shaft, but be careful not to trim so close as to damage the vanes. Generally, the short side of the vane was only used by old-time tiers, but depending on the location from which the wing (or tail feather) came, sometimes both vanes can be used.

Yallarhammer Collared

Hook: #10-16 Mustad 3399A
Thread: Black 6/0 Danville
Hackle: Split wing, dyed dove, quail, or starling
Body: Peacock herl
Weight: .015 to .025 lead wire (optional)

Yallarhammer Peacock Palmered

Hook: #10-16 Mustad 3399A
Thread: Black 6/0 Danville
Hackle: Split wing, dyed dove, quail, or starling
Body: Peacock herl
Weight: .015 to .025 lead wire (optional)

Yallarhammar

Hook:	#10-16 Mustad 9671
Thread:	Golden yellow
Tail:	Wood duck
Hackle:	Split wing, dyed dove, quail, or starling
Body:	Golden yellow floss
Weight:	.015 to .025 lead wire (optional)

Yallarhammar Dry

Hook:	#10-16 Mustad 94840
Thread:	Black 6/0 Danville
Tail:	Light ginger
Hackle:	Light ginger
Body:	Gold floss, palmered with split wing, dyed dove, quail, or starling

Yallarhammar Nymph

Hook:	#8-12 Mustad 3399A
Thread:	Yellow 6/0 Danville
Tail:	Grizzly dyed yellow hen hackles
Abdomen:	Bright yellow Uni-Floss
Thorax:	Peacock herl
Hackle:	Grizzly dyed yellow hen

Thunderhead

A handful of patterns that originated in and around the Great Smoky Mountains have garnered national attention, the Thunderhead among them. Universally attributed to Fred Hall, the Thunderhead was a result of Hall's admiration for the Adams and learning to apply Wulff-style kip-tail wings. His experimentation resulted in a buoyant, tough-as-nails pattern even the half blind such as me can see as it courses the currents of the park. Properly classified as an attractor-style pattern, the Thunderhead's features mimic those of a mayfly dun, matching with some accuracy everything from big quills to BWOs. I have found the pattern effective even when trout are keen on stoneflies and caddisflies. As with most fly-fishing success on these streams, presentation nearly always supersedes the need for precise imitation. Below is Fred Hall's recipe, along with two Johnny-come-lately variations known as the Thunderhead NC and Thunderhead TN.

Though many assume the pattern originated in the Southern Appalachians, according to some experts this fly actually had its beginnings out West. In the 1940s Jesse Jamerson of Lenoir City, TN, reportedly brought this pattern back from a trip to Wyoming. Jesse had his flies tied by Fred Hall in Bryson City, NC, and just like that word spread and the Thunderhead became popular in the Smoky Mountains.

Thunderhead (Fred Hall)

Hook: #10-18 Mustad 94840 or 94833
Thread: Black 6/0 Danville (pre-waxed)
Wing: White calf hair
Tail: Deer hair
Body: Gray dubbing
Hackle: Brown rooster neck

Thunderhead TN

Hook: #10-18 Mustad 94833
Thread: Gray 6/0
Wing: White calf hair
Tail: Brown hackle fibers
Body: Gray dubbing
Hackle: Grizzly cock

Thunderhead NC

Hook: #10-18 Mustad 94840 or 94833
Thread: Black 6/0 Danville (pre-waxed)
Wing: White calf hair
Tail: Deer hair
Body: Dark brown poly yarn
Hackle: Brown cock

Howell's Simple Bunny

Designed in 1998 by Kevin Howell of Davidson River Outfitters, Howell's Simple Bunny is the number-one streamer for catching trout, according Davidson's guide service records. Howell's Simple Bunny should be fished deep in the water column to be most effective. It's lethal whether you strip it slow or fast. The secret to the pattern is its exceptional lifelike movement in the water.

Hook: #2-8 Tiemco 9395
Thread: Black 6/0 UNI-Thread
Body: Cream-colored Zonker strip wrapped around hook shank
Over Wing: Dark-colored rabbit Zonker strip
Rib: UV Polar Chenille of desired baitfish color
Eyes: Medium lead dumbbell eyes painted red with black pupils.

Deer Hair Irresistible

Joe Messinger of Morgantown, WV, came up with the Deer Hair Drake. It was later renamed the Irresistible in the 1930s. Many variations of the Irresistible have appeared since Messinger tied his first fly, such as western North Carolina's Deer Fly and the Speck of east Tennessee. Ideal for rough water, the fly's spun deer-hair body provides great floatability on the waters of the Great Smoky Mountains.

Hook: #16 Tiemco 100
Thread: Black 6/0 Danville (pre-waxed)
Tail: Brown hackle fibers
Body: Spun clipped deer hair
Hackle: Brown
Head: Black silk

Carolina Wulff

The Carolina Wulff is a relatively recent addition to the Great Smoky Mountains fly pattern family and a direct offspring of the wildly popular Royal Wulff. Lee Wulff first tied the Royal and fished it with great success for decades. To my knowledge no one has laid claim to parenting the Carolina Wulff, which in the world of fly tying is something of an oddity. This buggy dry fly imitates many different types of mayflies and also terrestrials. A great dry fly for prospecting, the Carolina can be fished in slow or fast water.

Hook: #12-16 Mustad 94840 or 94833
Thread: Black 6/0 Danville (pre-waxed)
Wing: White calf hair
Tail: Deer hair
Body: Peacock herl with yellow color band
Hackle: Brown rooster neck or saddle

Tennessee Wulff

During the mid-1970s, the Tennessee Wulff found its way into fly boxes almost overnight. No one seems to know who first applied green to the normally red sections of the Royal Wulff. Other than the obvious difference in color, these flies are identical. As is the case on days when the trout here are finicky, one day the fish will prefer the red, and a day later they'll prefer the green. I am of the opinion that a number of tiers used green after Wulff-style wings came into wide use in the region. The pattern more or less showed up in fly shops in the area at about the same time with a number of tiers laying claim to having created it.

Hook: #12-16 Mustad 94840 or 94833
Thread: Black 6/0 Danville (pre-waxed)
Wing: White calf hair
Tail: Deer hair
Body: Peacock herl with chartreuse color band
Hackle: Brown rooster neck or saddle

Hillbilly Copper John

John Barr could not have realized the stir this pattern would create throughout the fly-fishing and tying world when he originated it in 1996. It steadily gained popularity and creditability among fly anglers all over the world. In 2001, this nymph pattern became the best-selling fly in the Umpqua catalog, joining the likes of other classic nymph patterns such as the Hare's Ear and Prince Nymph.

The popularity of the Copper John is not due simply to its good looks but rather to its uncanny ability to catch fish. Like other legendary fly patterns, this nymph has a few key features that make it appetizing. While the large gold bead, slim profile, flash, and breathing hackle are attractive, the fly's real strength comes from its weight. The compact design and special materials used in construction, such as the extensive copper body, allow this fly to sink quickly to the fish's level. This unique style of weighting a fly also allows it to naturally roll across the river bottom, more so than a fly weighted down with a split shot attached to the leader.

Hook: #14-20 curved nymph hook
Thread: Black 8/0
Bead: Brass bead to suit hook
Weight: Lead wire (.025")
Body: Copper wire
Tail: Black goose biots
Back: Clear flash straw; clear vinyl shell back
Thorax: Peacock herl
Legs: Partridge feather
Back: Epoxy

Woolly Worm

In the Great Smoky Mountains, the Woolly Worm is the perennial fish-anywhere go-to pattern. Its variations can be classified in almost any way. Some categorize the pattern as a wet fly, while others call it a nymph, and if you dress it up in drag, it will pass as a streamer pattern. Woolly Worms can be fished under the water surface or on it. In *Nymph Fishing for Larger Trout*, Charles Brooks recommended the Woolly Worm as a general-purpose nymph pattern. Tied in a variety of styles and colors, the Woolly Worm imitates an array of aquatic nymphs from stoneflies and dragonflies to damselflies and hellgrammites, not to mention terrestrial caterpillars. Who could ask for more?

Hook: #6-8 3XL Nymph
Thread: Black 6/0 UNI-Thread
Tail: Red wool
Body: Yellow chenille (medium)
Hackle: Cock neck grizzly

Gray Hackle Peacock

Perusal of Perrault's *Standard Dictionary of Fishing Flies* reveals there are almost two dozen variations in the Gray Hackle series. The regional favorite among these is the Gray Hackle Peacock, one of the earliest soft-hackle wet flies cast in the streams of the Great Smoky Mountains, perhaps as early as the 1840s. According to old records dating back to the beginnings of the sport, the pattern is said to be a yellow mayfly imitation with a trademark barred hackle that originated on the East and West Forks of the "Pegion" (now called Pigeon) River. Most agree, however, that the pattern resembles emerging caddis pupae. Some patterns withhold a thorax section and substitute the partridge for grizzly saddle hackle. By using a partridge hackle, a dubbed thorax will assist in supporting the hackle in an upright position. Partridge, having less web than the grizzly saddle hackle, imparts superior movement.

Hook:	#8-12 Mustad 3906B
Thread:	Black 6/0 UNI-Thread
Tag:	Gold tinsel
Tail:	Red hen hackles
UnderBody:	Black UNI-Yarn
Body:	Peacock herl (2 or 3)
Collar:	Grizzly saddle or hen neck hackles

The Deer Hair Fly

The Deer Hair Fly traces its ancestry back to western North Carolina around Lenoir and Bryson City, and some believe it was one of the first patterns in the region tied with clipped deer hair. Highly buoyant, the Deer Hair was a real go-to fly pattern in the 1950s and 1960s, but it fell from popularity in the 1970s, for reasons no one knows, to the point that it almost became a "dead pattern" unknown to the current generation of fly fishermen.

Hook: #8-12 Mustad 94840
Thread: Black 6/0
Wing: White calf body hair
Tail: Bear hair
Body: Spun deer body hair
Hackle: Brown neck

The Smith Fly

Bill Everhardt, an authority on the old trout-fly patterns of western North Carolina, alerted me to the Smith Fly, a very old pattern that hails from the Spruce Pine area of that state. It's fore and after hackling and orange body make it a dead ringer for October Caddis when they are plentiful on the streams. The pattern is listed in Everhardt's "Appalachian Series" at www.billeverhardt.com.

Hook:	#10-16 Mustad 94840
Thread:	Black 6/0
Wings:	Wood duck flank feathers
Tail:	Golden pheasant tippet
Butt Hackle:	Brown
Body:	Orange floss
Hackle:	Grizzly neck

The White Moth

An old fly pattern used for over seventy-five years by fly fishermen in western North Carolina, the White Moth is a godsend to older fly rodders who demand a fly that's easier to see, because its light color contrasts with dark water. The White Moth rides high and buoyant, but it is another nondescript pattern that has been around a long time just because it catches fish.

Hook: #10-16 Mustad 94840
Thread: White 6/0
Wings: White hackle tips
Tail: White deer hair
Body: White mink
Hackle: White
Weight: Copper wire (small)

Prince Nymph

Originated in 1941 by Doug Prince of Monterey, CA, the Prince Nymph has long been enormously popular among fly fishermen in the Great Smoky Mountains. It was initially called the Brown Forked Tail, and Prince actually used black ostrich herl instead of peacock herl in his original pattern. Peacock herl has a superior iridescence.

Keep in mind that the tail should be about half the shank length and the wings should extend from the head to the tail tie-in position. Both the tail and wing should have a narrow symmetrical angle so the wing tips are just beyond the width of the body. A nice variation is the CDC Prince Nymph, which uses CDC for the collar hackle. Other variations include: Mercer's Psycho Prince Nymph, GB Lite Brite Prince Nymph, TB Hotwire Prince, Fred Gordon's Prince Nymph, King Prince, Queen Prince, and Gold Bead Prince. Note that when purchasing fine gold Mylar, the material is silver on one side and gold on the other, but the silver faces out on the spool.

Hook: #10-16 Tiemco 10 or Daiichi 1180
Thread: Black 6/0 and 8/0
Bead: Gold-plated brass ⅛" with tapered hole
Wing: White goose biot
Tail: Brown goose biot
Body: Peacock herl
Rib: Gold Mylar (fine)
Hackle: Brown saddle
Weight: Lead wire (medium or small)

The Haystack

The Haystack is perfect to fish during spring mayfly hatches in the Great Smoky Mountains. You can easily tie this fly with materials found on virtually any fly-tying desk. You don't even need a hackle, and it floats extremely well in rough water. This old, traditional pattern is credited with inspiring the Compara-dun and Sparkle Dun. (In fact, look for hair labeled as Compara-dun hair when working on the wing and tail.) The Haystack is highly recommended by noted guide and fly tier Ian Rutter, who has authored several books on trout fishing in Tennessee and the Great Smoky Mountains.

Hook: #12-16 Mustad 94840
Thread: Yellow 6/0
Wing: Fine elk hair or deer body hair
Tail: Fine elk hair or deer body hair
Body: Superfine or other dry-fly dubbing

Orange Smoky Mountain Forked Tail

Sue Lundsford introduced me to the Orange Smoky Mountain Forked Tail, a very old east Tennessee fly. In the 1970s her father told me that he learned the pattern from the old timers in Cosby, TN. Many tiers and fly shop owners think the Orange Smoky Mountain Forked Tail is one of the earliest attempts at imitating the Sulphur. The materials used in this fly reflect some of the things available to fly fishermen in the early twentieth century. It's easy to tie, and is still a fish-catcher in the park.

Hook: #14 Mustad 94840
Thread: Orange floss
Tail: Brown goose biots (2)
Body: Orange floss
Wings: Tan goose biots (2)
Hackle: Light ginger cock

The Adams Family

The widespread use of the Adams family of flies in the park goes back at least seventy-five years, and it is a matter of enlightened conjecture as to how many old patterns such as the Jim Charley and Thunderhead morphed from the Adams. Although disputed to some degree, Charles F. Adams, an attorney from Lorain, OH, created the Adams patterns. The story goes that in the summer of 1922 he was fishing Mayfly Pond near Traverse City, MI, when he saw an insect that interested him. When he returned to his hotel, he described the insect to local fly tier Leonard Halladay. The account of what happened next was left to us by Halladay in a letter written some years later to fly-pattern historian Harold Smedley (Paul Schullery, "The Adams: 'A Great Salesman,'" *American Angler*):

> The first Adams I made was handed to Mr. Adams, who was fishing a small pond in front of my house, to try on the Boardman that evening. When he came back next morning, he wanted to know what I called it. He said it was a "knockout" and I said we would call it the Adams, since he had made the first good catch on it.

The following recipes cover the various patterns dubbed "the Adams Family" here. It is worth noting that some people believe that Fred Hall of Bryson City birthed the Adams Variant. This is unlikely, as the Adams Variant appears to show up in a number of other parts of the country at about the same time, although Hall probably was among the first in the region to tie this fly.

Adams Female

Hook:	#14-22 Mustad 94840
Thread:	Gray 8/0
Body:	Gray dubbing with yellow butt; use stretch floss or dubbing for butt
Tail:	Brown hackle barbs
Hackle:	Mixed cock (grizzly and brown)
Wing:	Grizzly hackle tips, hen or cock

Male Adams

Hook: #14-22 Mustad 94840
Thread: Gray 8/0
Body: Gray muskrat underfur
              dubbing
Tail: Brown hackle barbs
Hackle: Mixed grizzly and brown
Wing: Grizzly hackle tips, hen
              or cock

Adams Irresistible (Caddis)

Hook: #10-16 Mustad 94840
Thread: Black 6/0
Tail: Black, grizzly, or Coq
              de Leon
Body: Deer hair spun and
              clipped
Wing: Grizzly hen tips
Hackle: Grizzly and brown or Cree
Head: Black 6/0 thread

Adams Female Parachute

Hook: #12-22 Tiemco 100
Thread: Black 6/0
Tail: Grizzly and/or brown hackle fiber (stiff)
Body: Gray muskrat or dry-fly dubbing
Wing: Calf tail or poly yarn
Hackle: Brown and grizzly cock

Parachute Adams

Hook: #12-22 Tiemco 100
Thread: Black 6/0
Tail: Grizzly and/or brown hackle fiber (stiff)
Body: Gray muskrat or dry-fly dubbing
Wing: Calf tail or poly yarn
Hackle: Brown and grizzly cock

Adams Compara-dun

Hook:	#18-24 Tiemco 100 or 101
Thread:	Gray 6/0
Tail:	Black poly yarn or Antron
Body:	Gray UV dubbing
Wing:	Hareline Compara-dun elk hair

Adams Variant

Hook:	#12-16 Mustad 94840
Thread:	Black 6/0
Wings:	Grizzly hackle tips
Tail:	Golden pheasant tippet
Rear Hackle:	Grizzly
Body:	Yellow ostrich herl
Front Hackle:	Grizzly cock

Borcher Special

Aside from riding high in rough water and catching tons of wild trout in the Great Smoky Mountains, it's not really clear how a fly originating in Michigan became so popular here. Regardless, Ernie Borcher's pattern is a must for your fly bow. Although he used condor for the body of his personal flies, you'll do just fine with turkey. Most fishermen now use a parachute version.

Hook: #12-20 Mustad 94840
Thread: Black 6/0
Tail: Moose body hairs (3) or a few pheasant tail fibers
Body: Turkey tail fibers twisted and wrapped
Wings: Purple/maroon dyed hackle tips
Hackle: Brown and grizzly cock

Charlie's Whopper

One of the long-gone tiers of old, Charles C. Messer of western North Carolina was one of the first fly fishermen in the region to make a concerted effort to preserve the story of early fly patterns of the region. Charlie's Whopper is a robustly hackled sort of stimulator, part stone fly, part Pickett Fence–looking fly pattern, that is recommended for early spring. Whatever it was that Messer was seeking to imitate, he certainly created a fly that gets the attention of trout in these waters.

Hook:	#8-12 Mustad 94840
Thread:	Black 6/0
Wing:	Bronze mallard, upright and divided
Body:	Gray muskrat fur
Down Wing:	Bronze mallard
Hackle:	Grizzly and brown cock

Parmachene Belle

Used to varying degrees for 125 years in the Great Smoky Mountains, the Parmachene Belle, at first look, seems to be an unlikely pattern for this book. However, it was one of the first in the region, a fact that is well documented. Quoting *Fly Patterns and Their Origins* by Harold Hinsdill Smedley:

> This fly of Henry P. Wells, 1842–1904, by his admission, is his own child. This child, "born" about 1878, was named after Parmacheene Lake, in the Pine Tree State, Maine, favorite fishing locale of its father [Wells] when fishing for ouananiche [landlocked salmon]. Henry P. Wells, born in Providence, R.I., served in the invading Yankee army 1863-65, 13th N.Y. Artillery. The lake was name after Parmacheene, son of the Indian chief Metalluk.

The Parmachene was supposed to imitate the fin (belly) of a trout. There is no practical difference between this fly and the Gold Ibis. Like so many of the old and traditional flies there are many variations purported to be original. The late Dick Surette and Harold Hinsdill Smedley both give this dressing for the traditional Parmachene Belle.

Hook: #6-14 Mustad 3906
Thread: Black silk, monocord, or nylon
Tail: Red and white hackle barbules, mixed
Body: Yellow silk floss
Rib: Flat gold tinsel
Throat: Red and white hackle barbules, mixed
Wings: Married, red on tip (25 percent); white on bottom (75 percent)
Butt: Three or four turns peacock herl (optional)
Cheeks: Jungle cock

Wickham's Fancy Dry

I've included a small group of very old trout fly patterns in the book based solely on their use by the first generations of fly fishermen in the Great Smoky Mountains. Wickham's Fancy is one of them. Some of the oldest literature devoted to fly fishing for trout in the national park references this fly. Dr. T. C. Wickham, of Winchester, England, is credited with this fly. It suggests the Red Spinner in appearance, with wings of medium slate-gray starling and a body of gold tinsel over brown hackle, tied palmer. It is supposed to be particularly good when fish are "smutting" on the Test, a famous river in England.

Hook:	#14-16 Mustad 9671
Thread:	Brown 6/0
Tail:	Guinea fowl dyed reddish brown or ginger hackles
Body:	Flat gold tinsel
Rib:	Gold wire
Body Hackle:	Palmered ginger-red cock
Wing:	Medium starling wings set upright
Hackle:	Ginger-red cock

Trude

The Trude has a long history in the Great Smoky Mountain, as it's the first known to have been tied with hair as a substitute for feathers in the wings. It was created by Carter H. Harrison in 1903, while a guest on the A. S. Trude ranch in Idaho. According to the story, Harrison used red worsted from a rug for the body, added a bunch of hair from a red spaniel dog, and put it together with squirrel tail hackle on an oversize muskie hook. He presented it to Mr. Trude in fun. To the surprise of all, the fly proved to be a very effective pattern. The Royal Trude, a variation on the pattern, also has a long history of successful deployment on the waters of the Great Smoky Mountains.

Hook: #6-12 Mustad 94840
Thread: Black 6/0
Tail: Reddish-brown hackle fibers
Body: Scarlet wool yarn
Rib: Silver tinsel
Wing: Red fox squirrel tail
Hackle: Two reddish-brown neck or saddle hackles

Corey's Calf Tail

Although many regard the Corey's Calf Tail as a traditional southern Appalachian dry fly, it is actually a downsized version a Yankee pattern. Ralph Corey, who lived on the Muskegon in Lower Michigan, created the fly. His Calf Tails, which are down-wing dries, became widely popular after World War I. Corey tied the wings upright and divided of hair, and the patterns appeared almost simultaneously on the Beaverkill and the Ausable in New York around 1929. The fly made its way south, and has now been around so long that it has become an accepted member of the Great Smoky Mountain trout fly family.

Hook: #12-14 Tiemco 100 or 101
Thread: Tan 8/0 UNI-Thread
Wing: Calf tail
Tail: Calf hair
Body: Yellow dubbing
Rib: Brown feather
Hackle: Brown saddle

Jeff Wilkins's Tin Man Nymph

A gifted tier who is innovative by nature, Jeff Wilkins spent years experimenting with various materials to come up with a great leg material. He always used Flashabou accent or Krystal Flash (same material depending upon who is selling it) for many things, including legs. The material normally is a great accent for a body or tail, but I have recently been experimenting with it as leg material like Wilkins. It makes great terrestrial legs, dry-fly legs, dry-fly wing accents (especially caddis patterns), and nymph legs. In fact, the darker ones like olive, rootbeer, brown, or black make some of the best most durable "killer" nymph legs you will see. The Tin Man Nymph is a good pattern for imitating mayflies and caddis larvae and I recommend it for early-season emergences of big mayflies.

Hook:	#12-18 Daichii 1560
Thread:	Black UTC 70
Head:	Black brass bead (⁷⁄₆₄")
Tail:	Pheasant tail fibers
Abdomen:	Pearl Mylar tinsel, wrapped
Rib:	Small gold wire
Wing Case:	ThinSkin black (1 strip)
Legs:	Black Krystal Flash
Thorax:	Peacock herl

Early Nelson

The origin of the Early Nelson pattern is unknown. It's been around the region for at least seventy-five years, although its birthplace is a mystery. It was one of the first flies used before World War II by Cap Weise, who was a strong proponent. A popular school of thought suggests that the fly originated in England and came here via the Catskills as early as the 1840s. Those who subscribe to this history generally attribute the fly to Lord Nelson, who besides being a famous admiral of the Royal Navy was an ardent fisher of the chalkstreams of England. Weise was a well-read schoolmaster, so it is not unreasonable to think that he may have introduced the pattern to the region.

Hook: #10-16 94840 Mustad
Thread: 6/0 Black
Wing: Grizzly hackle tips
Tail: Moose or bear hair
Body: Peacock herl
Hackle: Grizzly and brown cock

Fore & After

Listed prominently in Roger's Lowe's popular *Fly Pattern Guide to the Great Smoky Mountains*, the Fore & After is an unusual dry-fly pattern that isn't often seen in fly boxes outside of the southern Appalachian region. Its pedigree is not known with any degree of accuracy, although many regard it as a western North Carolina original. This is Roger Lowe's recipe.

Hook: #12-18 Mustad 94840
Thread: Black 6/0
Tail: Golden pheasant
Body: Yellow dubbing floss
Hackle: Grizzly and brown cock

Hazel Creek

This old Smoky Mountain fly has been around for years, although I'm of the opinion that it's the brainchild of Roger Lowe of Waynesville, NC, at least in its modern form. I've seen several variations on the materials and colors used for this fly over the years. My best guess is that the Hazel Creek dates back to the 1960s, and perhaps not even that far back. Despite its inspiring name taken from the most famous of all streams in the Great Smoky Mountains National Park, no one has taken credit for the fly, nor is it found in any older fly lists. Nonetheless, this pattern is most effective in the late spring when the Sulphurs and Cahills are hatching.

Hook: #10-18 Mustad 94840
Thread: Light yellow 6/0 or 8/0
Wings: White hackle tips
Tail: Golden pheasant tippet
Body: Yellow dubbing
Hackle: Grizzly and brown cock, mixed

Jack Cabe Hopper

Created by Jack Cabe, a western North Carolina outfitter, the pattern is called a hopper, but I think it looks more like a caddis or a stonefly from underneath. It's an excellent searching pattern either way, and I have noticed few refusals. The Hopper is an extremely buoyant pattern that you can easily see in fast, broken water, and is a must for any well-armed fly fisherman frequenting the streams of the Great Smoky Mountains. The trick to getting the tail right is to use one grizzly and one brown hackle, each a size smaller than usual, as you will be tying in over the bunched kip-tail fibers, expanding the outer radius of the hackle.

Hook:	#10-16 Mustad 94840
Thread:	Black 6/0
Tail:	Red hackle fibers
Abdomen:	Molehair dubbing
Wing:	Light brown (dyed) kip tail, stacked
Hackle:	Grizzly (1) and brown (1)

Jim Charley

A number of us who invest time in looking up the origins of old fly patterns around the Smokies have tried in vain to pinpoint the originator of the Jim Charley fly pattern, and to my knowledge no one is sure of much other than that it's really old. This yellow mayfly attractor pattern is believed to have originated somewhere on the East and West Forks of the Pigeon River prior to World War II. Some knowledgeable experts attribute the fly to Charley Messer, but I'm unable to confirm this. Its barred ginger hackle is the Jim Charley's trademark.

Hook: #10-18 Daiichi 1180
Thread: Yellow 8/0
Tail: Medium ginger fibers
Body: Golden-yellow poly yarn
Wing: Barred medium ginger
Hackle: Ginger cock

Smoky Mountains Near Nuff

The Smoky Mountains Near Nuff (not to be confused with Dave Whitlock's Near Nuff series that includes his famous crayfish) is an old pattern with a checkered background, at least in terms of color and tying style. Roger Lowe lists the Near Nuff with a stripped grizzly quill-wrapped body that imitates a mosquito. I usually see this pattern tied with yellows and even browns. It is an excellent pattern for late-spring and early-summer fishing in the fast-flowing waters of the Great Smoky Mountains.

Hook: #14-18 94840 Mustad
Thread: Black 6/0
Wing: Wood duck, upright and divided
Tail: Grizzly hackle stems
Body: Stripped grizzly quill
Hackle: Grizzly cock

Orange Snipe

The Orange Snipe was originally created in Michigan, but found its way south into the Smokies through Frank Coffey of Maggie Valley, NC. By the late 1970s this pattern became very popular in western North Carolina and eastern Tennessee. According to master tier Roger Lowe, it's best to use these in the late summer and fall, tied on size 14 or 16 hooks. He suggests fishing the Orange Snipe dry on top water, just on the edge of the swift runs and seams for lots of action.

Hook: #10-16 Mustad 94840
Thread: Black 6/0
Wing: White hackle tips
Tail: Deer body hair
Body: Light orange poly yarn
Hackle: Grizzly and brown cock

The Smoky Mountain Palmer Clan

A pretty good argument could be made that the various versions of the Palmer Clan were the most widely used, and perhaps even most effective, fly patterns in the Great Smoky Mountains one hundred years ago. Palmer–style flies date back to before 1670, and are thought to have penetrated the Great Smoky Mountains by the 1840s, and certainly by the 1880s. Mark Cathey of Deep Creek loved the pattern, and the Cherokee used it considerably. References to Palmer flies of different colors appear frequently in literature on fly fishing in the Great Smoky Mountains. While the patterns are no longer as widely touted, I still highly recommend them for fishing here.

Palmer Orange

Hook: #10-16 Mustad 94840
Thread: Orange
Tail: Golden pheasant tail
Body: Orange poly yarn or dubbing
Hackle: Palmered brown and grizzly

Palmer Gray

Hook: #10-16 Mustad 94840
Thread: Black 6/0
Tail: Deer body hair
Body: Gray seal fur
Hackle: Palmered badger cock

Palmer Green

Hook: #10-16 Mustad 94840
Thread: Black 6/0
Tail: Deer body hair
Body: Green seal fur
Hackle: Green (dyed) palmered cock

Palmer Yellow

Hook: #10-16 Mustad 94840
Thread: Black 6/0
Tail: Deer body hair
Body: Pale yellow dubbing
Hackle: Palmered grizzly cock

Rattler

The Rattler is believed to have originated in western North Carolina in the 1970s, with a handful of tiers laying claim to its creation. I prefer to stay out of potential Hatfield/McCoy-level feuds—well, at least most of the time. I will say though, that the Rattler is a great variant-style dry-fly pattern fully capable of riding the swift, choppy waters of the Great Smoky Mountains. Its calf-tail wings make it an easily visible fly to follow.

Hook: #12-18 Mustad 94840
Thread: Black 6/0
Tail: Golden pheasant
Body: Black 6/0 thread, palmered brown saddle hackle
Hackle: Grizzly cock
Wings: White kip tail

Smoky Mountain Stimulator

The Stimulator is one of those flies that isn't so much a recipe but more of a starting pattern from which you can experiment with color to come up with different variations. Most tiers like to contrast yellow against orange dubbing. I have also seen peacock used in place of the dubbing, and even floss bodies will work. Stimulator variations are a bit like secret family barbecue sauces of the region. They are generally alike, but the ingredients can vary ever so decisively. The original Stimulator pattern is credited to Randall Kaufmann, a well-known fly fisher and writer who was seeking to imitate a large adult stonefly. However, it also works very well when caddisflies are active. Variations often fished in park waters include the Brown Stimulator, Stimulator Brown with Legs, Stimulator Olive, Stimulator Olive with legs, Stimulator Orange, Stimulator Royal, Stimulator Yellow, and Stimulator Yellow with Legs.

Hook: #6-16 Mustad 9671
Thread: Match body color
Tail: Light deer body hair
Body: Orange, olive, brown, or yellow poly palmered with ginger cock hackles
Thorax: Orange or yellow-dyed rabbit fur
Wing: Light deer hair at an angle over the body

Hot Creek Special

This volume would be grossly incomplete to overlook the flies developed by Don and Kevin Howell. Don passed away, but his son Kevin carries on at Davidson River Outfitters, ranking as the region's best-known expert with a fly rod, and also as a master fly tier. The Hot Creek Special was inspired by the ever-popular Zug Bug pattern; it came about when Kevin and Don were fishing the Nolichucky River's South Toe River arm in Yancey County, NC, during the dead of summer. The Howells rate it their number-one trout-catcher during late summer and autumn fishing.

Hook: #10-14 Mustad 3399
Thread: Black 6/0
Tail: Olive hackle fibers
Body: Peacock herl
Legs: Peacock herl
Back: Turkey quill

Bill's Provider

Another of the Howell clan's nationally known patterns is Bill's Provider. According to Don Howell, he received the pattern from Bill Hale of Anderson, SC. A longtime fly-fishing friend of Don's, Hale was fond of fishing Bitch Creek Nymph patterns. Bill's Provider has rubber legs and a more slender body than the Bitch Creek Nymph. Kevin Howell currently ties and sells this pattern at his fly shop in Pisgah, NC.

Hook:	#6-10 Mustad 9671
Thread:	Chartreuse 6/0 Eagle River
Rear Legs:	Brown rubber legs (medium)
Body:	Peacock herl
Front Legs:	Brown rubber legs (medium)

Howell Superfly

Don Howell developed this pattern at the suggestion of his fishing pal Renaud Pel-liter, who showed him a picture of a fly in an old issue of *Sports Afield*. His nymph pattern has since achieved widespread notoriety. A large stonefly nymph imitation, the Howell Superfly has proven itself from the slopes of the Rocky Mountains in Montana to the Great Smoky Mountains National Park.

Hook:	#2-10 Mustad 79580
Thread:	Camel UNI-Thread
Weight:	Lead wire (.030")
Tail:	Brown goose or turkey biots
Body:	Brown Swannundaze
Underbody:	Bright yellow wool or yarn
Wing Case:	Brown turkey tail
Legs:	Brown goose or turkey biots
Antennae:	Brown goose biots
Thorax:	Dubbed rabbit dyed ginger and picked

Kevin's Stone

When but a sprout in his father Don's fly-fishing business, Kevin Howell developed this well-known stonefly nymph pattern that has become universally known as Kevin's Stone. A great-looking fly, its exalted reputation is based on an ability to produce takes at a trout stream when just about everything else is ignored. The pattern has gained a national reputation for taking big trout from waters in the Rocky Mountains and Yellowstone to those of the Great Smoky Mountains.

Hook:	#8-12 Mustad 9671
Thread:	Black UNI-Thread
Weight:	Lead wire (.015" to .025")
Tail:	Brown goose biots
Abdomen:	Peacock herl
Back:	Brown turkey biot
Thorax:	Cream chenille palmered with grizzly cock
Legs:	Brown goose biots

Rex's Golden Stone

This book does not cover a lot of what most of us would term as modern innovations, as it is largely slanted to more traditional patterns. However, Rex's Golden Stone is included to demonstrate that even the region's most traditional tiers are current with cutting-edge fly-tying trends. Rex Wilson of Candler, NC, is a perfect example. He was mentored by one of the true old-time Smoky Mountains tiers, Frank Coffee. Having said this, Rex's Golden Stone features "prefabricated parts," and the application of ink from a Sharpie, something I am sure Horace Kephart would have loved to own when he was writing. Appearing sufficiently lifelike to crawl out of a fly box, Rex's Golden Stone is a great year-round prospecting fly for use in the waters of the GSMNP.

Hook: #8-10 Mustad 9672
Thread: Brown 6/0
Tail: Goose biots
Weight: Lead wire
Body: Latex
Thorax: Cabela's Soft-Shell Stone Bodies

Don's Pet

The stories behind the inception of many of the fly patterns developed by Don Howell are as interesting as the flies he created. Don's Pet is a great example. It came into being after Don and his brother, Dwight, lamented the lack of a dry-fly version of their Hot Creek Special pattern. Necessity is indeed the mother of invention, as quickly thereafter Don brought forth a dry-fly pattern he christened Don's Pet. He fashioned it as an attractor, but its effectiveness during hatches of green drake, both in the East and in the West, has become legendary.

Hook: #8-18 Mustad 94840
Thread: Black 6/0 UNI-Thread
Tail: Deer body hair (whitetail)
Back: Peacock herl
Rib: Silver #10 flat Mylar tinsel
Wings: Teal wing feathers
Hackle: Brown and grizzly, mixed

Don's Woven Nymph

One of the more complex patterns listed in this book, Don's Woven Nymph is yet another fly pattern created by the late Don Howell. Don always appreciated the trout-catching ability of woven nymph patterns, but he never liked the floss used to create these patterns. As the floss became tattered with use, the flies became progressively less productive. He discovered that patterns made with weaving chenille were more durable, but a bit too bulky. During a family visit, Don's niece showed him a project she was completing that involved the use of embroidery thread. Don adapted the material, and shortly thereafter he debuted Don's Woven Nymph.

Hook: #8-18 Mustad 9671
Thread: Light cahill 6/0 UNI-Thread
Tail: Chartreuse rubber legs (medium)
Wing Case: Black Swiss straw or mixed turkey tail
Thorax: Cream chenille
Wings: Chartreuse rubber legs (medium)

Pat's Nymph

In a sense this book is an outgrowth of L. J. DeCuir's book, *Southeastern Flies*. He picked up where I left off in the arena of providing information on old fly patterns used in the region, and I am picking up where he left off. His book chronicled fly patterns for use on southern waters, and devoted a chapter to flies with roots in the Great Smoky Mountains. One of his collaborators on the project was Pat Proffitt, a legendary fly fisherman and tier from Sevier County, TN. In those days Pat often worked as a guide on park waters for the Smoky Mountain Angler fly shop in Gatlinburg. Pat's Nymph is his creation. It is a substantially weighted pattern designed to allow anglers to plumb the depths of the fastest deep runs in these streams.

Hook: #6-16 Mustad 9671 or Tiemco 5262
Thread: Black 6/0
Weight: Lead wire (.025")
Tail: Brown and grizzly hackle fibers
Body: Muskrat dubbing
Hackle: Soft brown and grizzly saddle tied in a wet-fly collar

Miller Nymph

The Miller Nymph is another heavily weighted Pat Proffitt creation. It sinks fast and can be considerably effective when used with sinking fly line, although I have personally had success fishing two Miller Nymphs in tandem and using 40 to 50 feet of 4-pound monofilament line. For the tail, two goose biots should be tied forked, about one and a half times the hook gap in length. If you try this old nymphing technique you will be amazed at the volume of strikes you receive.

Hook: #6-16 Mustad 9671 or Tiemco 5262
Thread: Orange 6/0
Weight: Lead wire (.025")
Tail: Goose biots (2)
Body: Muskrat dubbing
Hackle: Brown saddle
Thorax: Muskrat dubbing

Ellison's Keel Hook Muddler Minnow

Compared with other types of flies, few streamer patterns appear to have deep roots in and around the waters of the Great Smoky Mountains National Park. Ellison's Keel Hook Muddler Minnow is an exception to this. Developed in the 1970s by Dave Ellison, former city engineer in Morristown, TN, this is a great fly that works well in winter and early spring. If pressed, it can be used as a grasshopper imitation as well.

Hook:	#1-4 Mustad 79666
Tail:	Red kip tail
Body:	Flat gold tinsel
Underwing:	Black kip tail
Wing:	Mottled turkey wing
Collar:	Deer hair
Head:	Spun deer hair

Ellison's Porter Creek Caddis

Few modern fly fishermen have spent as much time casting and studying the Greenbrier watershed in the GSMNP as Jim Ellison. He developed a number of fly patterns that were results of observation and experimentation there. His Porter Creek Caddis is a high-riding, extraordinarily easy-to-see pattern named after Porter Creek, a major Greenbrier tributary. Use this pattern between late spring and early summer for best results.

Hook: #10-18 standard dry fly
Thread: Light tan 8/0
Body: Very light tan dubbing
Hackle: White or light ginger, palmered
Wing: Light caribou (very light or white elk hair can be substituted

Little River Ant

This was the first terrestrial fly pattern I used in the Great Smoky Mountains. Its creator, Kirk Jenkins of Newport, TN, gave me several flies when we worked together in the early 1970s. He told me that he began tying them in the early 1960s. Since the pattern became popular, some tiers have altered it by adding a red rump. You'll often see "Little River Ants" for sale in fly shops around the Great Smoky Mountains, but notice that the tying style differs considerably from one to the next. It is deadly throughout the park during late summer to early winter when the terrestrials scurry about everywhere.

Hook: #12-20 Mustad 94840
Thread: Black 6/0 Danville
Body: Black ostrich herl
Hackle: Black cock

Cataloochee Copperhead

Over the years a lot of flies have been dubbed "copperheads" of some sort or another. The research I did on the name revealed a bevy of different patterns ranging from streams and wets to nymphs and emergers. This pattern is another brainchild of Kirk Jenkins. He also referred to it as the Honey Quill. In many ways the pattern is akin to the Red Quill, but Jenkins's twist on the pattern was to create it in a color that is more than a little reminiscent of the coppersnake, a pit viper that is quite common in the GSMNP.

Hook: #12-16 Tiemco 100
Thread: Black 70-denier UTC
Tail: Dark barred ginger
Body: Copper-colored quill
Wings: Wood duck
Hackle: Medium barred ginger

Black Parachute

Created by Mike Dennis of the Pisgah Chapter of Trout Unlimited in western North Carolina, the Black Parachute, according to its inventor, is irresistible: "The color black in a trout's diet is like dark chocolate is to me." So several years ago, Mike created the Black Parachute, even though he assumed that the fly already existed in some other iteration. I've searched exhaustively through fly books but I've never found this particular fly. It imitates ants, black midges, black mayflies, and other small black terrestrials. Mike's friend Bill Owen ties the Black Parachute with an orange post. The post is not an imitation of a wing but strictly a visibility aid for the fisherman.

Hook: #16-22 Mustad 94840
Thread: Black 6/0
Body: Black TCO East Coast Dubbing
Tail: Black hackles, equal to or less than the body length
Post: White or dyed-orange calf's hair

Pheasant Tail Parachute

The Pheasant Tail Parachute is not a traditional pattern of the GSMNP, but since parachute-style flies became popular in the 1980s, they have found their way into almost everyone's fly box. Just about all traditional dry fly-patterns fished in these waters now have a parachute variation. The reason is the effectiveness of this approach to hackling a dry fly. The parachute style of dry fly allows the fly's body to rest on the surface film, supported by the tail at the bend and the horizontally wound hackle up front. This hackle, since more fibers are in contact with the water's surface, is tied much sparser than standard dries, and typically the fibers are longer. There is no universally accepted origin of the parachute tying style, although we know that such flies were tied commercially in Scotland in the 1920s. In 1931, William Brush, a tier from Detroit, applied for a patent on the parachute hackle.

Hook: #12-16 Tiemco 5212
Thread: Black 6/0
Tail: Moose
Body: Ringneck pheasant tail
Hackle: Dark brown
Post: White kip tail
Rib: Gold wire

North Carolina Yellow Sally

One of the most important hatches to fly fishermen in the Great Smoky Mountains is the Yellow Sally stonefly emergence. Even a hundred years ago, Ernest Peckinpaugh listed the Yellow Sally among his commercially available patterns. The later versions he created for baitcasters had a half-ounce lead belly, more resembling a modern "V" spinnerbait without blades. The North Carolina Yellow Sally is a variation of the standard Yellow Sally, spruced up and customized by master tier Roger Lowe. It's a high-riding, trout-catching machine.

Hook: #10-18 Mustad 94840
Thread: Pale yellow 6/0
Body: Pale yellow dubbing
Wing: Bleached elk body hair
Thorax: Pale yellow dubbing
Hackle: Light blue dun

Little Green Stonefly

As best I can tell, no one knows much about the origins of the Little Green Stonefly in the Great Smoky Mountains. Most say, though, that they cannot recall a time when old timers didn't carry this pattern in their fly boxes. Bright apple-green stone-fly imitations have always been popular on these waters. Park waters are crawling—literally—with Green Stoneflies, and I haven't tried a pattern that tops this one. It's a bit high-tech in its material, but then Mother Nature offers little in the way of bright green furs or feathers.

Hook: #12-16 Mustad 94840
Thread: Green 6/0
Tail: Green poly yarn
Body: Green poly yarn
Hackle: Grizzly dyed green
Wing: Green poly yarn

Beadhead Hare's Ear Nymph

It is undocumented, but my gut feeling is that the traditional Hare's Ear Nymph patterns used so often by fly fishermen in the Great Smoky Mountains were the first flies upgraded to sport a flashy bead head. Traditional versions of the Hare's Ear Nymph pattern have been fished in these waters for at least a hundred years. The pattern has a buggy look about it that entices strikes wherever trout are found, and is most effective when fished deep. Prior to using bead heads, tiers relied on lead wire cores and even added lead split shots to the line and/or hook to get this productive pattern into the bowels of pools where the mossybacks lurk.

Hook:	#12-16 Mustad 3906
Head:	3⁄32" brass bead
Thread:	Brown 8/0
Tail:	Hare's ear guard hairs
Abdomen:	Hare's ear underfur
Thorax:	Hare's ear underfur and guard hairs, dubbed thick
Wing Case:	Mottled turkey quill section
Rib:	Oval gold tinsel

A. P. Nymph

There is some dispute about whether the name A. P. Nymph is derived from the fly's creator, Andre Puyan, who founded the first Trout Unlimited chapter in North Carolina, or if it stands for "All-Purpose" to describe its many uses. Puyan's fly can be tied in various shapes and sizes with several different types and colors of dubbing to mimic a variety of underwater insects. In creating the fly, Puyan reasoned that, although many nymphs are abundant in the stream, only certain types are available to trout, meaning the mobile types that swim and crawl within the trout's environment. He felt that muskrat and beaver (rather than hare's mask) were ideal materials for the proper texture to mimic gills along the abdomen and filaments along the abdomen and thorax of the most available nymphs.

Hook:	#12-18 Mustad 3906
Thread:	Gray, brown, black, or olive 6/0 or 8/0
Rib:	Gold or copper wire (fine)
Abdomen:	Gray, brown, black, or olive muskrat or beaver (or hare's mask) dubbing
Wing Case:	Dark moose hair
Tail:	Dark moose hair
Legs:	Dark moose hair
Head:	Gray, brown, black, or olive muskrat or beaver (or hare's mask) dubbing
Thorax:	Gray, brown, black, or olive muskrat or beaver (or hare's mask) dubbing

Little Yellow Sally Stonefly

The Little Yellow Sally Stonefly, from the family Perlodidae, measures about a quarter inch in size. These bright neon-yellow nymphs are quite abundant in the fast water of Great Smoky Mountains. The trout really love these little stoneflies, despite their size. The Yellow Palmer, which I believe was an early attempt to mimic the Yellow Sally Stonefly, was once one of the most popular patterns cast here. The Yellow Sally is a must for the fly box of anyone seeking success on these streams. The closed-cell foam is a modern addition to an ever-evolving pattern.

Hook:	#16 Tiemco 101
Thread:	Yellow 8/0
Body:	Yellow closed-cell foam
Wing:	Elk hair
Wing addition:	Pearl glister (5 strands)
Hackle:	Grizzly

Ellison's Greenbrier Special

Jim Ellison of Morristown, TN, is a gifted fly tier whose engineering background seeps into his efforts at the fly vise. His Greenbrier Specials are tied to imitate emerging caddis, which according to Jim are "greener than green" at Greenbrier. He trims the white hackle rib of his flies to within ⅟₃₂ inch of the spine. I defer here to his pattern instead of the more universally known Elk Wing Caddis, as they seem to be an awful lot alike. I cannot remember how many times I've had success over the years fishing the Greenbrier Special.

Hook: #12-18 TFS 100
Thread: Camel color 8/0
Body: Chartreuse Superfine dry-fly dubbing
Rib: White hackle
Hackle: Cream saddle
Wing: Elk hair, bleached

George Nymph

One of my heroes, Eddy George of Louisville, TN, created the George Nymph in 1955 after a trip to the Little River. He devised the first versions of this effective sub-surface fly pattern streamside, holding the hook in his hand as he tied. According to George, he cut and wrapped strips of lead to give the pattern weight before dressing it, a method he determined to be superior to putting a split shot on his leader, which was generally the custom in those days. Eddy added that the "cotton top" or "white hump" of the pattern was added to make the fly more visible in the fast water where stonefly nymphs are typically most available to trout. Today collections of flies tied by Eddy George are on display for all to see at Little River Outfitters fly shop and the Heritage Center in Townsend, TN, as well as at Bass Pro Shops in nearby Sevierville.

Hook:	#12-18 Mustad 94840
Thread:	Black 6/0
Weight:	Lead wire (.025")
Tail:	Brown hackles
Body:	Peacock herl
Hackle:	Brown cock
Thorax:	White rabbit fur dubbing
Wing Case:	Mottled white turkey quill

Greenbrier Girdle Bug

The Greenbrier Girdle Bug, an old standby western imitation of a stonefly, has earned itself a spot in the fly boxes of most local fly fishermen who have tried this killer pattern. This local variation is a modified version that uses a tungsten bead head to enable anglers to fish the deeper recesses of fast runs and narrow shuts. Many tiers still wrap the shank of the hook with a layer or two of lead wire, but most switch to a bead head once they compare the performance of the two at a stream. This is an excellent fly to use under a dropper during late winter through most of the spring.

Hook:	#8-12 Mustad 3906B
Thread:	Orange 6/0
Weight:	Tungsten bead head
Tail:	Rubber barred hackle
Body:	Orange variegated chenille
Legs:	Rubber barred hackle
Antennae:	Rubber barred hackle

C. K. Nymph

The background of the popular C. K. Nymph is pretty muddled. Is it a nymph you use as a crayfish imitation, or is it a crayfish imitation that you can use as a nymph? For years I understood the "C. K." to stand for Charles Knight, a noted fly tier in the 1960s from New York State. However, I've come upon some information suggesting the C. K. Nymph dates back to the late 1940s or early 1950s, originating, as the story goes, along the C. K. Williams stretch of the Bushkill Creek in Pennsylvania. C. K. Williams was the name of an old pigment production plant situated near the creek. Regardless of its provenance, the C. K. Nymph is a favorite among many guides in the Great Smoky Mountains. That is recommendation enough for me.

Hook: #6-12 Orvis 1524; Mustad 9671; Tiemco 5262
Thread: Rusty brown 8/0 UNI-Thread
Tail: Wapsi Marabou Golden Brown #MA050
Tinsel: Orange or equal Orvis Krinkle Mirror Flash
Body: Hareline Dubbin Hare'e Ice Dub Rusty Orange Dubbing
Hackle: Whiting Hebert Pro Grade brown saddle

Coffey's Creeper Stonefly

There's no question that western North Carolina tier Frank Coffey devised the popular Coffey's Creeper Stonefly. However, few agree on the general color of the pattern, which runs from strawberry blonde to dark brown throughout the region. It is not a matter of what is correct or incorrect, but which hue is most effective when and where you are casting this versatile stonefly nymph imitator.

Hook:	#8-14 Tiemco 3761 Nymph
Thread:	Brown 6/0
Weight:	Lead wire (.025")
Body:	Brown seal's fur
Rib:	Yellow 6/0 thread
Thorax:	Light hare's ear fur
Wing Case:	Molted turkey quills
Legs:	Wing case fibers turned beneath the body and trimmed

Tellico Nymph

If your fly box doesn't contain a Tellico Nymph, I will give you a couple. That's an easy offer for me to make, because if you're reading this, you probably have a supply of these flies stuck in various pockets of your fishing vest. Almost everyone loves and uses the Tellico Nymph. There is a general consensus that the pattern originated along the Tellico River in east Tennessee, and that these flies catch trout year-round. Other than that though, no one seems to agree about who tied the first Tellico Nymph, when it was created, or what it was intended to mimic.

I don't have the answers, although I have researched the matter, as did my old friend Eddy George, a Louisville, TN, native who is best remembered for his Cotton Top Nymph, a variation of the Tellico Nymph. George and I agreed that Ray Bergman was incorrect regarding the origins of the fly; he noted in the second edition of his book, *Trout*, that he credits its development to a Rev. Edwin T. Dalstrom of Tennessee. However, according to one source in North Carolina, the Tellico Nymph is an old pattern that was developed around 1927 by a priest along the Tellico River. Another source says that the Tellico Nymph was tied to imitate a kernel of corn.

I do know that Ernest Peckinpaugh was the first to offer the Tellico Nymph commercially. Based out of Chattanooga prior to World War I, Peckinpaugh was best known for his cork-bodied bass bugs, but he always offered trout flies as well. He sold his Tellico Nymphs—weighted and unweighted, and with and without Hildebrandt-style spinners—on cards in the 1940s.

The latest theory is that the original pattern is older than anyone has guessed. Some now say it was the effort of local fly tiers who crafted it from the McGinty wet fly around the turn of the twentieth century. I like the notion espoused here because the old timers of the Great Smoky Mountains were quite familiar with the McGinty pattern from their exposure to interloping Yankees fishing southern trout waters. Also worth noting is the fact that the McGinty was available by mail order from many sources. Like it or not, a lot of evidence suggests that most southern trout fly patterns of old were Yankee and European flies that influenced the earliest fly tiers of the Great Smoky Mountains.

If the origins of the Tellico Nymph are murky, the intent of its originator (other than catching trout) is just as muddled. For a number of years I was told it was a caddisfly larva imitation, which seemed logical enough to me as I had better success using Tellico Nymphs when caddisflies were hatching than at any other time. But these days I'm not so sure. A few experts note that the round body of the Tellico has a shape similar to mayfly crawler nymphs. Most of the mayfly nymphs in southern mountain streams are clingers and swimmers, but there are some crawlers. So I supposed it's possibly a mayfly nymph imitation.

There have been a number of legitimate variations of the Tellico. Author and tier Ian Rutter crafted an excellent rubber-legged version. There is also the much-used Green Tellico Nymph. Perhaps the best-known variation is the Blackburn Tellico Nymph. Richard Blackburn of Tennessee created it to imitate the Golden Stonefly nymphs that are common in the fast rocky streams of the Smokies. He has since relocated to Montana and taken his pattern with him.

Hook:	#4-12 Tiemco 5262
Thread:	Black 6/0
Tail:	Guinea fowl
Rib:	Peacock herl
Wing Case:	Turkey quill
Hackle:	Brown saddle
Body:	Yellow floss

Ellison's Tremont Banded Woolly Worm

If you are a fly fisherman with any experience at all on Southern Highlands freestone streams between mid-summer and late autumn, you know the importance of understanding the use of terrestrial fly patterns. In 2012 the popular patterns were those that mimicked cicadas, which were superabundant, as it was a peak year in the emergence of the 17-year locust. If they taught many fly fishermen a lesson, it is that big terrestrial flies catch big trout.

Jim Ellison, well known for his Greenbrier Caddis series, shared his version of a super-sized terrestrial, the Tremont Banded Woolly Worm, at the 2012 Troutfest in Townsend, TN. Ellison told me that for years he saw these big caterpillars along the streams of the Smokies, so he decided to tie an imitation. This variation of the traditional Woolly Worm is bigger and the band in the middle matches that of the naturals common in the Southern Highlands. It is weighted with #30 lead on both ends (⅛ inch of wraps on the front and back of the hook) to get it down where a big brown might be lurking.

Hook: #1 Dai-Riki 700
Thread: Brown or black 6/0
Body: Black (or, for reserves, brown) chenille
Hackle: Brown saddle

Horsehair Nymph

Unique to the fly boxes of anglers in the Great Smoky Mountains, this is not an old pattern as the name seems to imply, but a relatively modern arrival. Roger Lowe tied this pattern to imitate hellgrammites or stoneflies. Many anglers overlook the fact that hellgrammites are quite plentiful in the lower reaches of larger streams such as Little River, Abrams Creek, and the Little Tennessee River. The Horsehair Nymph's trademark is the wing case made with horse hair, giving it a distinct banded appearance that does an excellent job of mimicking the "edge" appearance of an ornery old hellgrammite. This is a buggy enough looking pattern that really produces well during the winter and early spring.

Hook: #4-12 Tiemco 5262
Thread: Black 6/0
Weight: Lead wire (.025")
Tail: Brown goose biots
Body: Peacock herl
Wing Case: Horse mane
Rib: Copper wire
Front Feeler: Brown goose biots

Blackburn Tellico Nymph

The best-known variation of the Tellico Nymph, this pattern was developed in the 1970s by Rick Blackburn, an east Tennessee fly fisherman and tier. Seeking to better imitate the large stoneflies found in the streams of the Great Smoky Mountains, he elongated the Tellico Nymph and gave it a slimmer profile. Currently living in Montana, he reports that his Blackburn Tellico Nymph pattern is as effective there as on the trout it was created to catch in his home waters of the southern Appalachian Mountains. Some tiers add a few rounds of lead wire to the shank to enable them to get this subsurface offering deeper than otherwise possible.

Hook:	#8-10 3XL to 2XL hook
Thread:	Dark brown
Tail:	Mink fibers or brown hackle fibers
Rib:	Peacock herl (2 strands)
Wing Case:	Dark brown turkey feather section
Body:	Dirty golden-yellow dubbing
Hackle:	Palmered through front half of body
Weight:	Lead wire (.010"), lightly wrapped

Cowdung Wet

Perhaps the oldest pattern listed in this book, Cowdung Wet actually preceded cows pastured in the Great Smoky Mountains. Of probable English descent, the Cowdung was a favorite of Izaak Walton and is often recommended in the earliest writings on trout fishing in the Southern Highlands. The larvae of these flies feed upon the excrement of cattle, and the females may be seen hovering in its vicinity as they lay their eggs near or upon it. The females are short-lived and do not wander, but the male flies prey upon smaller insects, especially tiny water flies, which they hold with their anterior feet while they suck the blood. In their greed they often venture too far, and fall into the water there they become a fat morsel for the waiting trout.

Hook: #8-14 Tiemco 5262
Body: Olive-green wool
Hackle: Brown saddle
Wing: Cinnamon (Orpington cock)

Zug Bug

Cliff Zug of West Lawn, PA, created the Zug Bug in the 1930s as a caddis fly imitation, and while it works well for that purpose it also works well as a prospector, dropper, and even as a wet fly on the swing. Easily one of the top ten nymph fly patterns of all time, the Zug Bug is a favorite of many fly fishermen knowledgeable of and experienced on the waters of the Great Smoky Mountains. It is most productive when fished in tandem as a dropper beneath a dry fly. The wing is best created with mallard flank tied over back and cut square midway down the shank.

Hook: #8-16 Tiemco 3761
Thread: Black 8/0
Body: Peacock herl
Tail: Peacock swords
Hackle: Brown hackle barbs, throat
Wing: Mallard flank
Rib: Oval silver tinsel

Lowe's Stone Nymph

Lowe's Stone, created by master tier Roger Lowe, is my personal favorite stonefly nymph to use in the Great Smoky Mountains. He noted that most stoneflies in the mountain streams where he guides have darker backs with lighter-colored underbellies, and he mimicked that coloration in this pattern. The trick to performing the task is to use latex for the body, and then apply dark spots with a permanent marker. He adds monofilament feelers to give the pattern an even more lifelike look in the water. Lowe's Stone is extremely effective when drifted in swift, broken stretches of water.

Hook: #6-12 9672 Mustad
Thread: Black 6/0
Weight: Lead wire (.025")
Tail: Dark Mono
Body: Latex, wrapped halfway down
Hackle: Grizzly cock, dyed brown
Feeler: Dark Mono

Red Fox Squirrel Hair Nymph

Dave Whitlock developed this pattern in the late 1960s and considers it one of his best nymphs. Using locally available red fox squirrel belly and back fur, he determined that air bubbles around these fibers gave the fly a distinct halo of liveliness and active movement in water. He now recommends a blend of squirrel fur and synthetic sparkle dubbing in a 60:40 ratio (natural to synthetic) for the abdomen and a 70:30 ratio for the thorax. Developed for use on the White River of Arkansas, this pattern is deadly in the Great Smoky Mountains as well as on a lot of other trout streams around the world.

Hook:	#6-16 Tiemco 5263
Thread:	Black 6/0 Danville
Weight:	Lead wire (.025")
Rib:	Oval gold tinsel
Abdomen:	Red fox squirrel abdomen dubbing
Tail:	Fox squirrel tail fibers
Thorax:	Red fox squirrel thorax dubbing
Legs:	Dark mottled partridge

My Pet

This is one of the oldest patterns I know of in the Great Smoky Mountains. I have also heard it called the Squash Bug by a number of old timers in the Cosby and Del Rio communities of Cocke County. Rotund versions of it were very popular in the 1970s when the major Japanese beetle infestation peaked in and around the national park. Due largely to the starkly simple, buggy look of the pattern, I think it perhaps predates the Tellico and certainly the George Nymph. It has been suggested that the pattern originated in the Newport, TN, area, but I don't put a lot of faith in such speculation. The pattern has definitely been around a long time, though. I wish we knew more about My Pet's origins, like so many other traditional patterns.

Hook:	#12-16 9672 Mustad
Thread:	Copper brown
Weight:	Lead wire (.025"); bead (optional)
Tail:	Deer body hair
Body:	Dark wool
Hackle:	Brown saddle
Wing Case:	Turkey tail quill

Pheasant Tail Nymph

The Pheasant Tail Nymph is rated the top year-round pattern by the majority of experienced anglers I have queried over the years on this subject. It mimics so many varieties of subsurface food for trout that it is almost always effective. Some sources credit the creation of the Pheasant Tail Nymph to Frank Sawyer, who fished the Wiltshire Avon in England. Sawyer's 1958 book *Nymphs and the Trout* describes his original recipe and tying method. However, the pattern is generally credited to Payne Collier, who was tying the Pheasant Tail Nymph in 1901. Regardless, the Pheasant Tail Nymph has been modified and redefined so many times that books could be written on just this one pattern. Popular variations for use in the waters of the park include adding a bead head and weighting the pattern by wrapping the shank of the hook with lead wire.

Hook:	#12-20 Tiemco 3761
Thread:	Black or brown 8/0
Weight:	Bead (optional)
Tail:	Pheasant tail (male)
Legs:	Pheasant
Body:	Pheasant
Rib:	Copper wire
Thorax:	Hare's ear
Wing Case:	Pheasant

Black Winter Caddis

When it's winter and there is snow on the ground, you can rely on the winter hatch of black/brown/olive winter caddis, also known as *Dolophilodes distinctus*. Sizes range from 18 to 22 (even smaller at times), and occur from December to March. This caddis also hatches midsummer, making it a unique bug in that it hatches during the winter and the summer months. Local tiers all appear to have their own designs for matching these small adults, but this is my favorite. For the body, double over 2 mm of brown foam, and segment the lower body with thread.

Hook: #18-22 Tiemco 2487
Thread: Brown 6/0 UNI-Thread
Body: Brown foam (2 mm)
Legs: Black saddle hen feather
Head: Mole dubbing

The Quill Gordon

This venerated fly pattern is the first dry fly that I ever tied. Just as Dad told me, it caught trout. The Quill Gordon has long been one of the most popular flies in the Smokies. Around the middle of March these mayflies begin hatching, often in big numbers, and some great emergences occur at lower elevations over the ensuing two weeks. Local tiers have long given their flies significantly more robust hackling than you'd find on the more traditionally tied versions from New York's Catskill Mountains. This is a necessary modification to make the pattern more buoyant on these rough southern streams.

Hook:	#10-16 Mustad 94831 or 94840
Thread:	Camel 8/0 UNI-Thread
Tail:	Light ginger spade hackle
Abdomen:	Tan or light brown dubbing with stripped peacock herl over it
Thorax:	Tan or light brown dubbing with stripped peacock herl over it
Hackle:	Light ginger cock

Red Bud

The Red Bud is Roger Lowe's variant of the older Gray Hackle Peacock pattern that he spiffed up by adding a brass bead head. Locals say it works best when the numerous redbud trees of the mountains are in bloom. I personally like the pattern and recommend it for use in the park during late winter and early spring.

Hook: #12-16 Mustad 9671
Thread: Black 6/0
Weight: Brass bead head
Tail: Red poly yarn
Body: Peacock herl
Hackle: Gray partridge

Blue-Winged Olive Sparkle Dun

Fly fishermen in the Great Smoky Mountains can encounter Blue-Winged Olives just about any time. Although BWOs are relatively small in size, many locals consider them the most important group of mayflies to look out for. You should not venture here without imitations of all stages of the BWO, but in my opinion, especially keep handy the BWO Sparkle Dun and the BWO Parachute. I carry all of the following: CDC Emerger, BWO Live Cripple, BWO Hackle Stacker, BWO Loop Wing Paradun, BWO Paranymph, BWO Parachute, BWO Fluttering Cripple, and BWO Pearl Wing Spinner. The list of BWO variations is almost infinite.

Hook: #18-22 Tiemco 100 or other standard TDE dry-fly hook
Thread: Olive, gray, or rust 8/0 UNI-Thread
Tail: Brown mayfly straight Z-Lon
Body: BWO Olive Superfine, Beaver, or Z-Lon dubbing
Wings: Medium gray or dyed dun coastal deer hair

Pink Lady

The Pink Lady is a very old pattern originally created to imitate "Pinkies"—duns of the *Epeorus* mayflies, which some refer to as Yellow Quills. The Pink Lady was the favorite fly of the famous author George La Branche in the early 1900s, who according to some visited the Great Smoky Mountains at least once. The story goes that La Branche stumbled on the recipe more or less by accident as he bought some King of Waters, a fly with a deep-red body that loses most of its color when fished, turning it pink. This striking pink fly features double-slip mallard quill wings. Today the Pink Lady is not used as often as it was fifty years ago, but it still produces and is certainly historically important to the story of fly fishing here. I can't remember the last time I lashed a Pink Lady onto a tippet, but I can assure you that at least one of the fly boxes I tote on these streams contains a couple of these lovely patterns.

Hook:	#10-16 Tiemco 3761
Thread:	White 6/0
Hackle:	Ginger hen
Wing:	Double-slip mallard quill
Rib:	Gold wire (fine) or tinsel (depending on fly size)
Abdomen:	Pink floss
Thorax:	Gray rabbit belly fur

Pale Sulphur Dun

While not particularly abundant in the Great Smoky Mountains, Sulphurs are one of my favorite hatches on these waters. Duns sit on the water surface after hatching longer than any other mayfly. They need to dry and to allow the blood to pump up to their wings. This process takes even longer in colder weather. On windy days, gusts can topple the drifting duns and drown them. If you don't see any rises for surface-floating duns during a hatch on windy days, the fish are subsurface feasting on the unlucky sinking drowned duns as well as on the emerging nymphs. Within twenty-four hours duns molt into spinners and are ready to mate. Males form mating swarms to attract females. When a female flies into the swarm she mates with a male. The spent males fall onto the water and drown. The females return to the riverside vegetation for a short period while the eggs mature. When the eggs are ready the females fly out over the water, dip into it, lay their eggs, and then fall spent into the water.

Hook: #14-18 Mustad 94831 or 94840
Thread: Yellow 6/0
Tail: Light dun hackles, divided
Body: Pale yellow dubbing
Hackle: Light dun cock
Wings: Light gray poly yarn, tied spent

Gray Hackle Yellow

One of the oldest patterns used in the Great Smoky Mountains, the wingless Gray Hackle Yellow has a well-deserved reputation for getting the attention of wild trout. It also may be the earliest dry fly used on these waters. Reminiscent of a sparsely dressed Catskill-style fly, the Gray Hackle Yellow has robust hackling to give it buoyancy. Slight to significant variations of this old-time pattern can be found on both sides of the Great Smoky Mountains.

Hook: #14-18 Mustad 94831 or 94840
Thread: Yellow floss
Tail: Red cock hackle barbs
Body: Yellow floss
Rib: Gold Mylar
Hackle: Grizzly cock

Green Weenie

The Green Weenie is one of the most celebrated flies to come out of the Great Smoky Mountains. Every year we get a monthlong trout feeding frenzy, as moth larvae burst onto the scene by the tens of thousands. Called green weenies, or inchworms, these tree-limb-rappelling caterpillars are everywhere along the stream. Trout gorge on green weenies through May, and well into summer and even beyond. These mountains hold multiple species of moth larvae ranging from 1 to 2 inches of protein-rich, green gummy goodness. When most of the trees have gotten the new year's foliage, you should start anticipating the hatch of the moth larvae.

Hook: #6-8 Tiemco 5262, MFC Wide Gap Curved 7181
Thread: Chartreuse 140-denier UTC
Underbody: .025" lead wire (¾ length of hook)
Legs: Chartreuse chenille
Body: Chartreuse chenille
Rib: 1X monofilament

Blue Dun

This classic trout dry-fly pattern, originated to imitate the early mayfly hatches, has been tied by generations of fly fishermen who know the streams of the Great Smoky Mountains. It's not a locally distilled pattern, but it has been around for a long time. These dry flies work for a number of hatches including Blue-Winged Olives, Hendricksons, Blue Quills, and Quill Gordons. The pattern seems to have fallen from favor over the last three decades, although it is still a solid choice with deep roots among traditional fly patterns of the Smokies.

Hook: #12-18 Mustad 94840, 94845, or 94833
Thread: Black 6/0
Body: Dubbed gray muskrat fur
Tail: Sparse blue dun barbules
Wing: Natural duck quill
Hackle: Medium blue dun

Groundhog Caddis

"Groundhog" is the local name for woodchuck, and shooting them has always been popular, although they are not nearly as tasty as either opossum or squirrel. Eric Leiser is credited with having popularized patterns using groundhog fur, and his highly buoyant, visible fly works more often than not. The pattern can be tied in various shades and hues to imitate a wide variety of caddisflies that inhabit the streams of the Great Smoky Mountains.

Hook: #10-16 Tiemco 100
Thread: Black 6/0 Danville
Body: Dubbing, applied thinly
Wing: Groundhog fur guard hairs
Legs: Brown cock hackle

October Caddis

The October Caddis in the Great Smoky Mountains is the "Isonychia of caddis hatches." As the fly's name implies, it emerges during the autumn months of October and November. These caddis can be quite prolific and are comparable in significance to major mayfly hatches. They are large aquatic insects that hatch sporadically at a number of streams, most notably at the nutrient-rich Abrams Creek. October Caddis primarily hatch at night into very early morning. It's best to fish this productive fly pattern early in the morning until noon, and then later at dusk. When working on the thorax, dub the mixed rusty orange rabbit and Z-Lon (or Antron) somewhat heavily; after a cast or two, the loose fibers will fall out, leaving a nice, fuzzy, floating thorax.

Hook:	#8-12 Tiemco 100
Thread:	Orange 6/0
Body:	Mixed rusty orange rabbit and Z-Lon (or Antron)
Underwing	Amber Z-Lon
Wing:	Orange-dyed elk body hair
Thorax:	Mixed rusty orange rabbit and Z-Lon (or Antron), touch-dubbed

Gray Fox

Many believe that the use of the Gray Fox, one of the old timers' favorites, preceded the arrival of the Adams. The Gray Fox mayfly pattern was originated by Catskills legend Preston Jennings. As a boy I discovered a first edition of Jennings's classic 1935 book *A Book of Trout Flies* in the Morristown library. The library was one of the few air-conditioned places we could ride our bikes to when the weather was really hot.

Jennings's book is one of the most cherished and highly regarded tomes in angling history. He was equally at home on the trout stream or in the lab. A highly regarded angler and fly tier, his work and contributions are legendary. Although the book dealt exclusively with streams in the Northeast, it was a real eye-opener for me. Developed as an eastern fly pattern, Jennings's Gray Fox has long been very effective in these southern waters, adequately matching lots of different mayflies from the March Browns to the Green Drakes.

Hook: #10-14 Tiemco 3761
Thread: Tan 8/0
Body: Tan or pale yellow dubbing (natural has pale yellow underbelly)
Tail: Ginger or brown hackle barbs
Hackle: Grizzly and ginger or brown cock
Wing: Wood duck
Rib: Brown 6/0 thread (optional)

March Brown Wet

The March Brown imitates the March Brown mayfly, or *Rithrogena germanica*, which is Latin for "big fat hairy fly." It's not all that common in the waters of the Great Smoky Mountains, but you will encounter them in late winter and early spring. I find the pattern to be more productive on bigger than on smaller waters. It's been used in the park for well over seventy-five years. The pattern is most effective when fished as a dropper under a dry fly or a nymph. Be sure that when you are nymphing with this pattern that you let it swing up at the end. This imitates how these large insects swim up to the surface to hatch.

Hook: #10 Tiemco 3761
Thread: Camel 8/0 UNI-Thread
Tail: Barred mallard flank, dyed wood duck fibers
Body: Yellow/tan caddis East Coast Dubbing
Rib: Heavy brown cotton thread
Wing: Mottled turkey tail
Hackle: Ruffed grouse

Muskrat Nymph

Developed many years ago and credited to Polly Rosborough, a Washington-based fly tier who was given the Buszek Award for his innovative patterns, the Muskrat Nymph is an adaptable "buggy" pattern like those that caught on long ago among fly fishermen in the Great Smoky Mountains. The Muskrat Nymph is an easy fly to tie and many different local versions of the pattern exist. According to the pattern's proponents, muskrat fur is somewhat distinctive among natural folics in that it retains tiny air bubbles in the fibers.

Hook: #12-18 Mustad 9671
Thread: Black 6/0 or 8/0
Tail: Black spade hackle fibers mixed with muskrat fur
Abdomen: Muskrat dubbing
Thorax: Black ostrich herl
Legs: Black hackle tied beard-style

Stickbait

If you grew up around any of the old timers who fished these waters, you can recall that the mere utterance of "stickbait" made them smile. Yes, it's the nickname of the caddisfly pupa, and this family of aquatic insects is well represented in the waters of the Great Smoky Mountains. As with so many "updated" patterns, today you get latex at fly shops, which is the correct color and texture for imitating many species of caddis pupa.

Hook: #10-18 Mustad 3906
Thread: Gray 6/0
Weight: Brass bead head
Body: Thin latex
Thorax: Gray rabbit dubbing

Montana Nymph

As the name implies, the Montana Nymph is a purely western pattern, but you will often find it carried in the locals' fly arsenals. The waters of the Great Smoky Mountains are prime stonefly habitat, and this Big Sky State native is mighty effective. Oddly, it was first tied by a New Yorker, Lew Oatman. I mention it here mostly to benefit visiting fly fishermen, as everyone is familiar with the pattern and you can even buy it at Walmart. One thing is certain: the Montana Nymph has caught a lot of trout on the waters here. This is the traditional recipe for the Montana Nymph.

Hook:	#6-12 Daiichi D1270 3XL Nymph
Thread:	Black 6/0
Tail:	Black hackle fibers
Body:	Black chenille
Weight:	Lead wire (.010")
Thorax:	Yellow chenille
Thorax cover:	Black chenille
Hackle:	Black saddle

Apple Green Caddis (Emerger)

One of the first insects in these waters that caught my eye was the bright green caddisfly. This is the best pattern for mimicking these bugs when they are the focus of trout. I have found that the pattern works best at elevations over three thousand feet, but I can only guess why this has been true in my experiences. Prior to the arrival of "bead technology," I tied this pattern (along with about everything else that I fished below the surface) with a few wraps of lead around the shank of the hook. Bead heads not only look better, they are a lot faster to apply.

Hook: #14-18 Gateway S300
Thread: Brown 8/0
Body: Apple-green dubbing
Hackle: Partridge, sparse
Wing: Dark dun CDC
Head: Brown dubbing

Ramsey (or Brown Hackle)

The Brown Hackle probably predates the medieval fly list of Dame Juliana Berners, and it is noted in many of the earliest references to recommended flies of the Great Smoky Mountains. Ernest Ramsey of Middle Creek in Sevier County, TN, used to supply Brown Hackle wets that he called Ramsey Flies. He told us that his uncle, who guided fishermen there before 1900 (and who was also a noted keeper and trainer of gamecocks), tied the pattern and frequently used it. It's a pretty nondescript pattern that often worked well, but it was never one of our go-to flies.

Hook: #10-14 Mustad 94831
Thread: Black 8/0 UNI-Thread
Tail: Golden pheasant tail tippets
Tag: Gold Mylar tinsel
Body: Peacock herl
Hackle: Brown cock

Guinea

I was amazed the first time I hunted guinea fowl in Africa, as I grew up in the sticks of east Tennessee thinking that they were not much different from chickens. African guinea fowl are wild, free-ranging fowl that are hunted for sport much the same as grouse are hunted in the U.S. Guinea fowl in east Tennessee are domesticated. Where I grew up, everyone had a chicken coop where everything from bannies to guineas roosted at night. Early tiers here had ample access to guinea plumage, which I suppose is the most logical explanation for the pattern being unknown pretty much anywhere else. According to Roger Lowe, the pattern looks like the small golden stoneflies found in these streams, and the guinea feathers provide a lifelike appearance.

Hook:	#12-16 Mustad 9672
Thread:	Black 6/0
Tail:	Guinea
Body:	Light tan poly yarn
Wing Case:	Dark brown poly yarn
Rib:	Black floss
Legs and Feelers:	Guinea

Leadwing Coachman Wet

One of the earliest flies noted in Great Smoky Mountain fishing literature, the Leadwing Coachman's origins go back to the early 1800s, supposedly when an English carriage driver offered it to his lord for fishing. The Leadwing Coachman can still be an effective fly today. Its peacock herl body has shown up as an attractor on many patterns, including the Zug Bug and the Prince Nymph. The best time to use the Leadwing Coachman is during gray caddisfly hatches, particularly when dry flies seem to be ineffective. The Leadwing looks like diving caddis laying its eggs on the bottom of the trout stream.

Hook: #8-12 Tiemco 9300
Thread: Black 6/0 Danville
Tail: Gold pheasant tippets
Rib: Gold wire (fine)
Body: Peacock herl
Wings: Mallard quills
Hackle: Ginger/brown saddle

Grizzly King

For better or worse, my selection of flies for this book was influenced by data gathered from the earliest writings about fishing in the Great Smoky Mountains. While barely a footnote to the sport today, the Grizzly King and a handful of other oldies were the go-to flies of generations past. Professor James Wilson, brother of John Wilson (creator of the Professor fly), crafted this pattern. In his 1840 book *The Rod and the Gun*, James Wilson describes his fly:

> The Grizzly King is a hackle par excellence. They call him Coomberland in the northern parts of merry England. His wings are broad and burly, formed of any undyed feather, bearing narrow natural bars of black and white, and he bristles with many stripes from head to heel, his dark green body being wound about with gray or mottled hackle, and terminated by a fiery tail, turned up in what naturalists call an ensiform manner—that is, somewhat after the fashion of a sword. What seems his head, the likeness of a kingly crown has on.

I've included this handsome old-time fly more for its historical significance than its present-day popularity.

Hook: #6 Mustad 3399
Thread: Black 6/0
Tail: Red wool yarn
Body: Green silk
Rib: Gold wire
Wing: Mallard breast
Hackle: Plymouth Rock, palmered

Joe's Hopper

There's a score or two of great hopper imitations used in the Great Smoky Mountains, but none are as widely used or more respected than Joe's Hopper. A sort of standard-bearer, this terrestrial insect pattern was developed by Art Winnie of Traverse City, MI, in the early 1940s; it was originally called the Michigan Hopper. It wasn't until well-known fly-fishing writer Joe Brooks popularized it in the 1950s that the pattern got its current name. Local tiers have a fondness for customizing their own versions of this pattern, as they can be especially creative with the various shades of green. There is also a significant movement today among many local tiers to substitute foam for the traditional wool yarn and chenille used to construct the body of this terrestrial deceiver.

Hook: #4-16 Tiemco 5212
Thread: Black or dark brown
Body: Yellow wool or chenille
Wings: Turkey quill sections (2)
Tail: Red hackle fibers or deer hair
Rib: Brown hackle
Hackle: Brown and grizzly mixed

Griffith's Gnat

Griffith's Gnat is a very good general-purpose fly when midges or any other small aquatic insect are being preyed upon by trout. You can fish the fly static or on a varied retrieve using a floating line. The palmered grizzly hackle allows the fly to ride atop the surface. George A. Griffith, the founder of Trout Unlimited, invented his namesake Gnat, whose simple design and common tying materials produce one of the world's most effective dry flies.

Hook: #18-24 Tiemco 101
Thread: Olive or black 8/0 or smaller
Body: Peacock herl
Hackle: Grizzly palmered
Rib: X-fine gold wire, optional to strengthen herl

Humpy

Californian Jack Horner came up with the Humpy in the 1940s, and it was first known as Horner's Deer Hair Fly. At some point during that decade, the term "Humpy" was attributed to it, and the name stuck. Boots Allen, the owner of a small fly shop in Jackson Hole, WY, is thought to have come up with it. The Humpy was an instant success when it reached the South in the early 1950s, and it is certainly one of the most successful attractor flies created. Many variations have evolved from it, the most popular being the Yellow Humpy, which can be used to imitate Little Yellow Sallies and small Golden Stoneflies. Western fly-tying legend Jack Dennis changed the traditional deer-hair body to elk hair in the 1960s, and I used his pattern with great success after reading his book.

Hook:	#12-14 Tiemco 100
Thread:	Black 3/0 Danville monocord
Body:	Deer hair
Shellback:	Deer hair
Tail:	Deer hair
Wing:	Deer hair

Elk Hair Caddis

I would be completely remiss to omit the Elk Hair Caddis as one of the top patterns fished in the Great Smoky Mountains. It is on everyone's top-five flies list. The Elk Wing Caddis was developed by Al Troth somewhere in the middle of the last century and has become a favorite all across the country. Local tiers create the pattern in light and dark versions, some using deer hair and some using caribou. The results seem pretty much the same: the trout can't resist this high-riding pattern no matter what time of year it is.

Hook:	#12-14 Tiemco 100SPBL
Thread:	Tan, brown, olive, or black 8/0 UNI-Thread
Rib:	Gold wire
Abdomen:	Yellow, caddis green, or tan dubbing
Thorax:	Yellow, caddis green, or tan dubbing
Hackle:	Brown rooster neck

Brown Bivisible

There has always been some debate in and around the Great Smoky Mountains if the overtied palmer-hackled flies—such as the Leadwing Coachman—fathered the popular Bivisible family, or if the Bivisibles are just Yankee patterns that have been adapted locally. At any rate, the Bivisibles' pedigree is not very well known or acknowledged. Nevertheless, the venerable patterns have been cast here for almost a century, but if you want to make a point about it, it's not really from around here. The Bivisible first shows up in print in 1926, when Edward Ringwood Hewitt wrote in his book *Telling on the Trout*:

> Dark colors are more visible to the trout from below than light colors, and, there-fore, take more fish under most conditions and are more generally used. They are often, however, more difficult to see on the water than the lighter flies. This is the reason for my favorite design of fly which I call the Bi-Visible which consists of a palmer-tied brown hackle on the head of which is wound a small wisp of white hackle. The white resting against the brown becomes very visible in most lights to the angler; on the other hand, the trout see the brown hackle from below better than any other color used. This fly is by far the best of any I have yet seen for all species of trout and it is based on a sound physical principle.

Years later Hewitt claimed at least partial credit for the creation of the pattern, noting:

> The Brown Bivisible with the white wisp at its head, which I myself introduced, although palmer flies somewhat similar had been in use for many years in England. The white wisp enables the angler to see the fly readily, hence the name I gave it—Bivisible because I can see it and the trout can see it. The fly in various sizes is certainly the most universally useful fly we have, and is perhaps more fished now than any other dry fly. Palmer flies are made in various colors and are called Bivisibles in tackle stores, but this is incorrect. The true Bivisible is brown, with a white wisp of feather at its head.

Despite not originating locally, the Brown Bivisible has always produced well in the waters of the Great Smoky Mountains.

Hook: #10-18 Mustad 3906
Thread: Black 8/0
Tail: Brown hackle
Body: Brown cock hackle, 2 to 3 wraps of white hackle at the collar

American Express

The American Express is a modern pattern of renown created by Wayne Clodfelter, editor of the newsletter, *Trout, NC*. A dry-fly pattern derived from the basic concept of the Parachute, the fly's poly post wing design not only enhances its buoyancy in turbulent mountain streams, but it also makes it easier to see. It projects a tempting silhouette to trout lurking in deeper water, and the color combination is irresistible to trout in the Smokies.

Hook: #14-22 Tiemco 9230 or 900BL
Thread: Tan 6/0 UNI-Thread
Tail: Brown cock hackles, tied split
Body: Medium tan Spectrablend dubbing
Wing: Tan polypropylene, posted

Infallible

A devoted hunter, trapper, conservationist, fly tier, and skilled angler, Cato Holler is a Tarheel State legend who regularly saved the fur and feathers from his activities and turned the material into fine flies. His favorite was the one he named Infallible. The dark-hued pattern works well during late winter through late spring. Holler was the first recipient of the Senior Lifetime Sportsman's license, a certificate he received when he was eighty-five years old and lived on Lake Tahoma, not far from his property on Armstrong Creek. An episode of *American Sportsman* starring Lee Wulff and Grits Gresham was filmed on his private section of Armstrong Creek in the 1970s.

Hook: #10-14 Tiemco 9230 or 900BL
Thread: Tan 6/0 UNI-Thread
Tail: Badger tail guard fibers
Body: Mink fur dubbing
Wing: Wood duck (flank feather)
Neck: Brown cock hackle

Bust-A-Brown

One of the best websites you can visit about fly fishing for trout in the South is David Perry's www.southeasternfly.com. Besides being a talented, knowledgeable writer, Perry has also devised a number of innovative patterns over the last two decades. His top taker for fishing in the Great Smoky Mountains is a wet-fly pattern he christened the Bust-A-Brown. According to David the pattern evolved on his vise while he was experimenting with soft-hackle tying techniques. The result has so far racked up an impressive catch record on tough waters—such as Little River—in the Great Smoky Mountains.

Hook:	#10-12 Tiemco 9300
Thread:	Black 6/0 Danville
Tail:	Squirrel tail
Rib:	Green tinsel and copper wire (fine)
Body:	Peacock herl

Kevin's Caterpillar

Kevin Howell designed this big pattern to imitate bagworms or tent caterpillars commonly found in the Southeast. These woolly caterpillars often build their hornet's-nest-size tent houses over streams and emerge in clusters bigger than your fist. Many of them fall into the water where trout and bass relish them. According to Davidson River Outfitters, Kevin's Caterpillar is one of their top-selling and producing flies from July to late October. For a properly trimmed hackle, make sure it's clipped to be no more than $\frac{1}{16}$ inch above the peacock herl. On larger versions of this fly, a foam underbody will help build bulk and keep the fly afloat. Use a yarn underbody if you want to sink the fly.

Hook:	#8-12 Tiemco 2302
Thread:	Black 6/0 UNI-Thread
Body:	Peacock herl
Hackle:	Ginger straw Whiting saddle, sized to the gap of the hook
Underbody:	Yarn
Legs:	Peacock herl
Rib:	Black wire XS

G. Neil Daniels Fly

This interesting little fly was designed by the late Don R. Howell of Brevard, NC, for George Neil Daniels, a lifelong bachelor attorney from Greensboro. Daniels used the pattern extensively for catching bream, but also found it deadly on southern trout. According to the story, the fly morphed with instructions for slight changes from Daniels to Howell from an odd-looking little "Woolly Worm" given to Neil by an Indian guide during a fishing trip to Canada. For the pattern pictured here, clip the hackle with a slight taper so that it resembles a football: fat in the middle and thin at each end. The hackle should be equal to the gap of the hook at the high point. The pattern is still commercially available from Davidson River Outfitters.

Hook: #8-12 Tiemco 5262
Thread: Black 6/0 UNI-Thread
Body: Black and white varigated chenille
Hackle: Black strung saddle

Reuben Wood

Bill Everhardt lists the Reuben Wood in his "Appalachian Series" of trout flies. When I asked him about this, he told me the fly was used extensively by the old timers, and to the best of his knowledge it was of unknown, but western North Carolina origins. As it turns out the fly is described in Mary Orvis Marbury's *Favorite Flies and Their Histories*. It is named after Reuben Wood, a legendary nineteenth-century angler. In the early 1900s Wood fly fished with the biggest guns, including the famous fishing writers and authorities Charles Orvis, Seth Green, and Theodatus Garlick. Here is Everhardt's recipe, which judging from the color plates in Marbury's book, appears to be dead-on.

Hook: #8-14 Mustad 94840
Thread: Black 6/0
Tail: Mallard flank feathers
Body: White chenille with red floss tip
Wing: Mallard flank feathers
Hackle: Brown cock neck

Kay's Mink Fly

I regard Bill Everhardt's Kay's Mink Fly as a classic, if for no other reason than because of its origins. According to its creator, his wife, Kay, allowed him to snipe a bit of underfur from her mink coat. Doubtless Benny Joe Craig, who was known for finding fly-tying material in odd places like old furs and fur coats, would have been impressed. Kay's Mink Fly is reminiscent of the Gray Fox, an old pattern with a long history on the waters of the Great Smoky Mountains.

Hook: #8-14 Mustad 94840
Thread: Black 6/0
Tail: Bear hair
Body: Dubbed mink fur
Wings: Grizzly hackle tips
Hackle: Black cock

Stanley's Grizzly

Stanley Tuttle of Lenoir, NC, is credited with creating this simple yet highly productive fly pattern. Stanley, an old-school tier who learned to create flies pretty much on this own, called this his "killer fly." It is an effective year-round pattern that can be fished like a wet fly or stripped like a streamer. Tuttle also created a popular dry-fly pattern known as the Tiger Tail.

Hook: #8-12 Mustad 9671
Thread: Black 6/0
Tail: Grizzly bear fiber
Body: Cream dubbing palmered with fine copper wire
Wings: Grizzly cock hackle
Weight: Lead wire (.011")

John's Woolly Worm

One of several Woolly Worm variations noted in this book, this particular pattern was created by John Turner of Lenoir, NC. According to some, he was among the first around the Great Smoky Mountains to apply rubber-band legs to flies. When fishing this fly on the surface, Turner would give it a twitch for better results. It worked for him for many years—he stream-fished into his late eighties.

Hook: #10-14 Mustad 94831
Thread: Black 6/0
Legs: White rubber bands
Body: Black dubbing with grizzly and brown palmered hackles

Legg's Extended Body Inchworm

A relatively new pattern designed by Tyler Legg, his Extended Body Inchworm (EBI) floats like a cork and can withstand abuse from a large trout's teeth. It's a perfect small-stream fly, where fish usually only take one swing at a dry. They'll rise several times to the EBI if the first time doesn't do it. Cast the EBI under overhanging brush for the best results. It's quite visible, even when pulled under the surface by currents. I have applied some gel floatant to the Inchworm, but it may not really be necessary.

Hook: #4-10 Mustad 94831
Thread: Chartreuse 6/0
Legs: White rubber bands
Body: Cork

Acknowledgments

As much as I might hope to cover all the bases, it's impossible to note everyone who helped make this book possible—I am just too scattered-brained. There's dozens of people who know more about the subject than I do, so I am humbled to been able to put this information together. This represents the efforts of many people who share a passion for fly fishing the waters of the Great Smoky Mountains National Park.

Many of the flies in this book were tied for me by David Erikson of Birmingham, Alabama. A quiet guy with an irrepressible smile, David can be found at the Deep South Outfitters in Birmingham—at least when he's not fly fishing. An expert fly tier, David provided most of the flies pictured in the book. For this and his support and friendship, I am very grateful.

Joel Dean of Tennessee Traditional Flies also gets a hardy thank you, as does Roger Lowe of Brookings Fly Shop and Kevin Howell of Davidson River Outfitters. Bill Everhardt's help was indispensible as were the contributions of Rex Wilson, Ron Gaddy, David Perry, Walter Babb, Jeff Wilkin, Byron Begley, and Jim Ellison. Again, the common dominator of these people is that they all share a love of fly fishing in the Great Smoky Mountains.

Bibliography

Almy, Gerald. *Tying and Fishing Terrestrials*. Mechanicsburg, PA: Stackpole Books, 1978.

Altman, Heidi M. *Eastern Cherokee Fishing*. Tuscaloosa: The University of Alabama Press, 2006.

Bartram, William. *William Bartram, 1739–1823, Travels through North and South Carolina, Georgia, East and West Florida*. Cambridge, UK: Cambridge University Press, 2011.

Bergman, Ray. *Trout*. Second edition. New York: Alfred A. Knopf, 1952.

Brown, Mac. *Casting Angles: A Fly Casting Handbook*. Bryson City, NC: Highland Press, 1997.

Camuto, Christopher. *A Fly Fisherman's Blue Ridge*. New York: Henry Holt and Company, 1990.

Cantrell, Mark A. *The Fishes Gathered in Cherokee Country*. Asheville, NC: U.S. Fish and Wildlife Service for the Eastern Band of Cherokee Indians, 2005.

Casada, Jim. *Fly Fishing in the Great Smoky Mountains National Park: An Insiders Guide to A Pursuit of Passion*. Rock Hill, SC: High Country Press, 2009.

Cash, Bo. *Water Under the Bridge*. Swannanoa, NC: Brushy Mountain Publishing, 2011.

DeCuir, L. J. *Southeastern Flies*. Birmingham, AL: Menasha Ridge Press, 2000.

Dickey, Charley, and Fred Moses. *Trout Fishing*. Birmingham, AL: Oxmoor Press, 1972.

Fears, J. Wayne. *Trout Fishing the Southern Appalachians*. Charlotte, NC: East Woods Press, 1979.

Fish, Frederic F. *Trout Fishing Waters of North Carolina*. Raleigh, NC: The Graphic Press, 1971.

Gasque, Jim. *Hunting and Fishing in the Great Smokies*. New York: Alfred A. Knopf, 1948.

Hall, J. E. B. *Western North Carolina Fly Guide*. Swannanoa, NC: Brushy Mountain Publishing, 2007.

Harris, William Charles. *Angler's Guide Book and Tourists' Gazetteer of the Fishing Waters of the United States and Canada, 1885.* New York: American Angler, 1885.

Hewitt, Edward Ringwood. *Telling on the Trout.* New York: Scribner, 1930.

Holler, Cato Oliver. *Adventures of a Lifetime: The Autobiography of an American Sportsman.* Old Fort, NC: Hollow Hills Publishing, 1998.

Howell, Don, with contributions from Kevin Howell. *Tying and Fishing Southern Appalachian Trout Flies.* Clayton, GA: Fern Creek Press, 1999.

Hunnicutt, Samuel J. *Twenty Years Hunting and Fishing in the Great Smoky Mountains.* Maryville, TN: Byron's Publishers, 1951.

Jacobs, Jimmy. *Tailwater Trout in the South: An Angler's Guide.* Woodstock, VT: Backcountry Publications, 1996.

———. *Trout Streams of Southern Appalachia: Fly-Casting in Georgia, Kentucky, North Carolina, South Carolina & Tennessee.* Woodstock, VT: Backcountry Publications, 1994.

Jennings, Preston J. *A Book of Trout Flies.* New York: Derrydale Press, 1935.

Kirk, Don. *Fly-Fishing Guide to the Great Smoky Mountains.* Birmingham, AL: Menasha Ridge Press, 1996.

———. *Smoky Mountains Trout Fishing Guide.* Revised edition. Hillsborough, NC: Menasha Ridge Press, 1985.

———. *Smoky Mountains Trout Fishing Guide.* Dayton, OH: McGuire Denton Publishers, 1981.

Kirk, Don, and Greg Ward. *The Ulitimate Fly-Fishing Guide to the Great Smoky Mountains.* Birmingham, AL: Menasha Ridge Press, 2011.

La Branche, George. *The Dry Fly and Fast Water Fishing with The Floating Fly on American Trout Streams.* New York: Derrydale Press, 2000.

Lanman, Charles. *Adventures in the Wilds of North America, Volume 2.* Memphis, TN: General Books, 2012.

Lawrence, H. Lea. *The Fly Fisherman's Guide to the Great Smoky Mountains National Park.* Nashville, TN: Cumberland House, 1998.

Leeson, Ted, and Jim Schollmeyer. *Trout Flies of the East.* Portland, OR: Frank Amato Press, 1999.

Lincoln, Robert Page. *Black Bass Fishing: Theory and Practice.* Mechanicsburg, PA: Stackpole Books, 1952.

Lowe, Roger. *Roger Lowe's Fly Pattern Guide to the Great Smoky Mountains: 101 Traditional Fly Patterns.* Privately printed for author in 2012.

———. *Smoky Mountain Fly Patterns.* Waynesville, NC: Smoky Mountain Graphics, 1992.

Manley, Joe F. *Fishing in the Great Smoky Mountains National Park and Adjacent Waters.* Gatlinburg, TN. Vanity published, 1938.

Marbury, Mary Orvis. *Favorite Flies and Their Histories.* Boston: Houghton Mifflin, 1892.

Mason, Robert L. *The Lure of the Great Smokies*. Nabu Press, 1927.

Moseley, Bill. *Trout Fishing in the North Carolina Mountains*. Chicago: Adams Press, 1986.

Moses, Fred, and Charley Dickey. *Charley Dickey & Fred Moses Trout Fishing*. Birmingham, AL: Oxmoor House, 1975.

Rutter, Ian. *Great Smoky Mountains National Park Angler's Companion*. Portland, OR: Frank Amato Publications, 2002.

———. *Tennessee Trout Waters: Blue-Ribbon Fly-Fishing Guide*. Portland, OR: Frank Amato Publications, 2003.

Rutter, Ian, and Charity Rutter. *Rise Rings & Rhododendron: Fly Fishing the Streams and Tailwaters of Southern Appalachia*. Townsend, TN: Thunderhead Press, 2006.

Sawyer, Frank. *Nymphs and the Trout*. UK: Sawyer Nymphs, Ltd., 1952.

Schullery, Paul. "The Adams: 'A Great Salesman.'" *American Angler*. October 4, 2007. Accessed: February 5, 2014. http://www.americanangler.com/history/a-great-salesman.

Snelling, Ken. *A Smoky Mountains & Southern Appalachians Fly Hatch Schedule*. Knoxville, TN: Graphic Spirit, 1994.

Wayment, Andrew Marshall. *Heaven on Earth: Stories of Fly Fishing, Fun & Faith*. American Book Publishing, 2012.

Wilson, James. *The Rod and the Gun*. London: A. and C. Black, 1840.

Zeigler, Wilbur Gleason. *The Heart of the Alleghanies*. Raleigh, NC: A. Williams & Co., W. W. Williams, 1883.

Index